Emmet Scott
LaPorte Ind
2 - 13 -'15   AEJ

THE UNKNOWN GUEST

The Unknown Guest

BY

MAURICE MAETERLINCK

Translated by

ALEXANDER TEIXEIRA DE MATTOS

NEW YORK

DODD, MEAD AND COMPANY

1914

TRANSLATOR'S NOTE

Of the five essays in this volume, *The
Knowledge of the Future* has appeared in
the *Cosmopolitan Magazine,* of New York,
The Elberfeld Horses in the *Metropolitan
Magazine,* of the same city, and *The Unknown Guest* in *Harper's Magazine.* The
remainder have not, at this present date,
been published elsewhere.

A. T. DE M.

CHELSEA, 20*th June,* 1914.

CONTENTS

INTRODUCTION

I

MY ESSAY on *Death*[1] led me to make a conscientious enquiry into the present position of the great mystery, an enquiry which I have endeavoured to render as complete as possible. I had hoped that a single volume would be able to contain the result of these investigations, which, I may say at once, will teach nothing to those who have been over the same ground and which have nothing to recommend them except their sincerity, their impartiality and a certain scrupulous accuracy. But, as I proceeded, I saw the field widening under my feet, so much so that I have been obliged to divide my work into two almost

[1]Published in English, in an enlarged form, under the title of *Our Eternity* (London and New York, 1913).—*Translator's Note.*

Veridical, of hallucinations which take place simultaneously with and are True representations of happenings elsewhere

equal parts. The first is now published and is a brief study of (veridical) apparitions and hallucinations and haunted houses, or, if you will, the phantasms of the living and the dead; of those manifestations which have been oddly and not very appropriately described as "psychometric"; of the knowledge of the future: presentiments, omens, premonitions, precognitions and the rest; and lastly of the Elberfeld horses. In the second, which will be published later, I shall treat of the miracles of Lourdes and other places, the phenomena of so-called materialization, of the divining-rod and of fluidic asepsis, not unmindful withal of a diamond dust of the miraculous that hangs over the greater marvels in that strange atmosphere into which we are about to pass.

2

When I speak of the present position of the mystery, I of course do not mean the

Introduction

mystery of life, its end and its beginnings, nor yet the great riddle of the universe which lies about us. In this sense, all is mystery, and, as I have said elsewhere, is likely always to remain so; nor is it probable that we shall ever touch any point of even the utmost borders of knowledge or certainty. It is here a question of that which, in the midst of this recognized and usual mystery, the familiar mystery of which we are almost oblivious, suddenly disturbs the regular course of our general ignorance. In themselves, these facts which strike us as supernatural are no more so than the others; possibly they are rarer, or, to be more accurate, less frequently or less easily observed. In any case, their deep-seated causes, while being probably neither more remote nor more difficult of access, seem to lie hidden in an unknown region less often visited by our science, which after all is but a reassuring and con-

ciliatory expression of our ignorance. To-
day, thanks to the labours of the Society
for Psychical Research and a host of other
seekers, we are able to approach these phenomena as a whole with a certain confidence. Leaving the realm of legend, of
after-dinner stories, old wives' tales, illusions and exaggerations, we find ourselves
at last on circumscribed but fairly safe
ground. This does not mean that there are
no other supernatural phenomena besides
those collected in the publications of the
society in question and in a few of the more
weighty reviews which have adopted the
same methods. Notwithstanding all their
diligence, which for over thirty years has
been ransacking the obscure corners of our
planet, it is inevitable that a good many
things escape their notice, besides which the
rigour of their investigations makes them
reject three-fourths of those which are
brought before them. But we may say

Introduction

that the twenty-six volumes of the society's *Proceedings* and the fifteen or sixteen volumes of its *Journal,* together with the twenty-three annuals of the *Annales des sciences psychiques,* to mention only this one periodical of signal excellence, embrace for the moment the whole field of the extraordinary and offer some instances of all the abnormal manifestations of the inexplicable. We are henceforth able to classify them, to divide and subdivide them into genera, species and varieties. This is not much, you may say; but it is thus that every science begins and furthermore that many a one ends. We have therefore sufficient evidence, facts that can scarcely be disputed, to enable us to consult them profitably, to recognize whither they lead, to form some idea of their general character and perhaps to trace their sole source by gradually removing the weeds and rubbish which for so many hundreds and thou-

sands of years have hidden it from our
eyes.

3

Truth to tell, these supernatural manifestations seem less marvellous and less
fantastic than they did some centuries ago;
and we are at first a little disappointed.
One would think that even the mysterious
has its ups and downs and remains subject
to the caprices of some strange extramundane fashion; or perhaps, to be more exact,
it is evident that the majority of those
legendary miracles could not withstand the
rigorous scrutiny of our day. Those which
emerge triumphant from the test and defy
our less credulous and more penetrating
vision are all the more worthy of holding
our attention. They are not the last sur-
vivals of the riddle, for this continues
to exist in its entirety and grows greater
in proportion as we throw light upon it;

but we can perhaps see in them the supreme or else the first efforts of a force which does not appear to reside wholly in our sphere. They suggest blows struck from without by an Unknown even more unknown than that which we think we know, an Unknown which is not that of the universe, not that which we have gradually made into an inoffensive and amiable Unknown, even as we have made the universe a sort of province of the earth, but a stranger arriving from another world, an unexpected visitor who comes in a rather sinister way to trouble the comfortable quiet in which we were slumbering, rocked by the firm and watchful hand of orthodox science.

4

Let us first be content to enumerate them. We shall find that we have table-turning, with its raps; the movements and transportations of inanimate objects without contact; luminous phenomena; *lucidité,* or clairvoyance; veridical apparitions or hallucinations; haunted houses; bilocations and so forth; communications with the dead; the divining-rod; the miraculous cures of Lourdes and elsewhere; fluidic asepsis; and lastly the famous thinking animals of Elberfeld and Mannheim. These, if I be not mistaken, after eliminating all that is insufficiently attested, constitute the residue or *caput mortuum* of this latter-day miracle.

Everybody has heard of table-turning, which may be called the A B C of occult science. It is so common and so easily produced that the Society for Psychical Research has not thought it necessary to devote special attention to the subject. I need hardly add that we must take count only of movements or "raps" obtained without the hands touching the table, so as to remove every possibility of fraud or un-

Introduction

conscious complicity. To obtain these movements it is enough, but it is also indispensable that those who form the "chain" should include a person endowed with mediumistic faculties. I repeat, the experiment is within the reach of any one who cares to try it under the requisite conditions; and it is as incontestable as the polarization of light or as crystallization by means of electric currents.

In the same group may be placed the movement and transportation of objects without contact, the touches of spirit hands, the luminous phenomena and materializations. Like table-turning, they demand the presence of a medium. I need not observe that we here find ourselves in the happy hunting-ground of the impostor and that even the most powerful mediums, those possessing the most genuine and undeniable gifts, such as the celebrated Eusapia Paladino, are upon occasion—and the occasion occurs but too often—incorrigible cheats. But, when we have made every allowance for fraud, there nevertheless remains a considerable number of incidents so rigorously attested that we must needs accept them or else abandon all human certainty.

The case is not quite the same with levitation and the wonders performed, so travellers tell us, by certain Indian jugglers. Though the prolonged burial of a living being is very nearly proved and can doubtless be physiologically explained, there are many other tricks on which we have so far no authoritative pronouncement. I will not speak of the "mango-tree" and the "basket-trick," which are mere conjuring; but the "fire-walk" and the famous "rope-climbing-trick" remain more of a mystery.

The fire-walk, or walk on red-hot bricks or glowing coals, is a sort of religious ceremony practised in the Indies, in some of the Polynesian islands, in Mauritius and elsewhere. As the result of incantations uttered by the high-priest, the bare feet of the faithful who follow him upon the bed of burning pebbles or brands seem to become almost insensible to the touch of fire. Travellers are anything but agreed whether the heat of the surface traversed is really intolerable, whether the extraordinary power of endurance is explained by the thickness of the horny substance which protects the soles of the natives' feet, whether the feet are burnt or whether the skin remains untouched; and, under present conditions, the question is too uncertain to make it worth while to linger over it.

"Rope-climbing" is more extraordinary. The juggler takes his stand in an open space, far from any tree or house. He is accompanied by a child; and his only *impedimenta* are a bundle of ropes and an old canvas sack. The juggler throws one end of the rope up in the air; and the rope,

as though drawn by an invisible hook, un-
coils and rises straight into the sky until
the end disappears; and, soon after, there
come tumbling from the blue two arms, two
legs, a head and so on, all of which the wiz-
ard picks up and crams into the sack. He
next utters a few magic words over it and
opens it; and the child steps out, bowing
and smiling to the spectators.

This is the usual form taken by this particular sorcery. It is pretty rare and seems
to be practised only by one sect which origi-
nated in the North-West Provinces. It has
not yet perhaps been sufficiently investigated to take its place among the evidence
mentioned above. If it were really as I
have described, it could hardly be explained
save by some strange hallucinatory power
emanating from the juggler or illusionist,
who influences the audience by suggestion
and makes it see what he wishes. In that
case the suggestion or hallucination covers

Introduction

a very extensive area. In point of fact,
onlookers, Europeans, on the balconies of
houses at some distance from the crowd of
natives, have been known to experience the
same influence. This would be one of the
most curious manifestations of that "unknown guest" of which we shall speak
again later when, after enumerating its acts
and deeds, we try to investigate and note
down the eccentricities of its character.

Levitation in the proper sense of the
word, that is to say, the raising, without contact, and floating of an inanimate object or even of a person, might
possibly be due to the same hallucinatory power; but hitherto the instances
have not been sufficiently numerous or authentic to allow us to draw any conclusions.
Also we shall meet with it again when we
come to the chapter treating of the materializations of which it forms part.

CHAPTER I

PHANTASMS OF THE LIVING
AND THE DEAD

THE UNKNOWN GUEST

CHAPTER I

PHANTASMS OF THE LIVING AND THE DEAD

I

THIS brings us without any break to the consideration of veridical apparitions and hallucinations and finally to haunted houses. We all know that the phantasms of the living and the dead have now a whole literature of their own, a literature which owes its birth to the numerous and conscientious enquiries conducted in England, France, Belgium and the United States at the instance of the Society for Psychical Research. In the presence of the mass of evidence collected, it would be absurd to persist in denying the reality of the phenomena themselves. It is by this time incontestable that a violent or deep emotion can be transmitted instantaneously from one mind to another, however great the distance that separates the mind experiencing the emotion from the mind receiving the communication. It is most often manifested by a visual hallucination, more rarely by an auditory hallucination; and, as the most violent emotion which man can undergo is that which grips and overwhelms him at the approach or at the very moment of death, it is nearly always this supreme emotion which he sends forth and directs with incredible precision through space, if necessary across seas and continents, towards an invisible and moving goal. Again, though this occurs less frequently, a grave danger, a serious crisis can beget and transmit to a distance a similar hallucination. This is what the S. P. R. calls "phantasms of the living." When the hallucination takes place some time after the decease of the person whom it seems to evoke, be the interval long or short, it is classed among the "phantasms of the dead."

The latter, the so-called "phantasms of the dead," are the rarest. As F. W. H. Myers pointed out in his *Human Personality*, a consideration of the proportionate number of apparitions observed at various periods before and after death shows that they increase very rapidly for the few hours which precede death and decrease gradually during the hours and days which follow; while after about a year's time they become extremely rare and exceptional.

However exceptional they may be, these apparitions nevertheless exist and are proved, as far as anything can be proved, by abundant testimony of a very precise character. Instances will be found in the

Proceedings, notably in vol. vi., pp. 13-65, etc.

Whether it be a case of the living, the dying, or the dead, we are familiar with the usual form which these hallucinations take. Indeed their main outlines hardly ever vary. Some one, in his bedroom, in the street, on a journey, no matter where, suddenly sees plainly and clearly the phantom of a relation or a friend of whom he was not thinking at the time and whom he knows to be thousands of miles away, in America, Asia or Africa as the case may be, for distance does not count. As a rule, the phantom says nothing; its presence, which is always brief, is but a sort of silent warning. Sometimes it seems a prey to futile and trivial anxieties. More rarely, it speaks, though saying but little after all. More rarely still, it reveals something that has happened, a crime, a hidden treasure of which no one else could know. But we will return to these matters after completing this brief enumeration.

2

The phenomenon of haunted houses resembles that of the phantasms of the dead, except that here the ghost clings to the residence, the house, the building and in no way to the persons who inhabit it. By the second year of its existence, that is to say, 1884, the Committee on Haunted Houses of the S. P. R. had selected and made an analysis of some sixty-five cases out of hundreds submitted to it, twenty-eight of which rested upon first-hand and superior evidence.[1] It is worthy of remark, in the first place, that these authentic narratives bear no relation whatever to the legendary and sensational ghost-stories that still linger in many English and American

[1] *Proceedings*, vol. i., pp. 101-115; vol. ii., pp. 137-151; vol. viii., pp. 311, 332, etc.

magazines, especially in the Christmas numbers. They mention no winding-sheets, coffins, skeletons, graveyards, no sulphurous flames, curses, blood-curdling groans, no clanking chains, nor any of the time-honoured trappings that characterize this rather feeble literature of the supernatural. On the contrary, the scenes enacted in houses that appear to be really haunted are generally very simple and insignificant, not to say dull and commonplace. The ghosts are quite unpretentious and go to no expense in the matter of staging or costume. They are clad as they were when, sometimes many years ago, they led their quiet, unadventurous life within their own home. We find in one case an old woman, with a thin grey shawl meekly folded over her breast, who bends at night over the sleeping occupants of her old home, or who is frequently encountered in the hall or on the stairs, silent, mysterious, a little grim.

Or else it is the gentleman with a lack-lustre eye and a figured dressing-gown who walks along a passage brilliantly illuminated with an inexplicable light. Or again we have another elderly lady, dressed in black, who is often found seated in the bow-window of her drawing-room. When spoken to, she rises and seems on the point of replying, but says nothing. When pursued or met in a corner, she eludes all contact and vanishes. Strings are fastened across the staircase with glue; she passes and the strings remain as they were. The ghost—and this happens in the majority of cases—is seen by all the people staying in the house: relations, friends, old servants and new. Can it be a matter of suggestion, of collective hallucination? At any rate, strangers, visitors who have had nothing said to them, see it as the others do and ask, innocently:

"Who is the lady in mourning whom I met in the dining-room?"

-If it is a case of collective suggestion, we should have to admit that it is a subconscious suggestion emitted without the knowledge of the participants, which indeed is quite possible.

Though they belong to the same order, I will not here mention the exploits of what the Germans call the *Poltergeist,* which take the form of flinging stones, ringing bells, turning mattresses, upsetting furniture and so forth. These matters are always open to suspicion and really appear to be nothing but quaint frolics of hysterical subjects or of mediums indulging their sense of humour. The manifestations of the *Poltergeist* are fairly numerous and the reader will find several instances in the *Proceedings* and especially in the *Journal* of the S. P. R.

As for communications with the dead, I devoted a whole chapter to these in my essay entitled *Our Eternity* and will not return to them now. It will be enough to recall and recapitulate my general impression, that probably the dead did not enter into any of these conversations. We are here concerned with purely mediumistic phenomena, more curious and more subtle than those of table-rapping, but of the same character; and these manifestations, however astonishing they may be, do not pierce the terrestrial sphere wherein we are imprisoned.

3

Setting aside the religious hypotheses, which we are not examining here, for they belong to a different order of ideas,[1] we find, as an explanation of the majority of

[1] On the same grounds, we will also leave on one side the theosophical hypothesis, which, like the others, begins by calling for an act of adherence, of blind faith. Its explanations, though often ingenious, are no more than forcible but gratuitous asseverations and, as I said in *Our Eternity,* do not give us the shadow of the commencement of a proof.

these phenomena, or at least as a means of avoiding an absolute and depressing silence in regard to them, two hypotheses which reach the unknown by more or less divergent paths, to wit, the spiritualistic hypothesis and the mediumistic hypothesis. The spiritualists, or rather the neospiritualists or scientific spiritualists, who must not be confused with the somewhat over-credulous disciples of Allan Kardec, maintain that the dead do not die entirely, that their spiritual or animistic entity neither departs nor disperses into space after the dissolution of the body, but continues an active though invisible existence around us. The neospiritualistic theory, however, professes only very vague notions as to the life led by these discarnate spirits. Are they more intelligent than they were when they inhabited their flesh? Do they possess a wider understanding and mightier faculties than ours? Up to the present, we have not the unimpeachable facts that would permit us to say so. It would seem, on the contrary, if the discarnate spirits really continue to exist, that their life is circumscribed, frail, precarious, incoherent and, above all, not very long. To this the objection is raised that it only appears so to our feeble eyes. The dead among whom we move without knowing it struggle to make themselves understood, to manifest themselves, but dash themselves against the impenetrable wall of our senses, which, created solely to perceive matter, remain hopelessly ignorant of all the rest, though this is doubtless the essential part of the universe. That which will survive in us, imprisoned in our body, is absolutely inaccessible to that which survives in them. The utmost that they can do is occasionally to cause a few glimmers of their existence to penetrate the fissures of those singular organisms known as mediums. But these vagrant, fleeting, ven-

turous, stifled, deformed glimmers can but
give us a ludicrous idea of a life which
has no longer anything in common with the
life—purely animal for the most part—
which we lead on this earth. It is possible;
and there is something to be said for the
theory. It is at any rate remarkable that
certain communications, certain manifestations have shaken the scepticism of the cold-
est and most dispassionate men of science,
men utterly hostile to supernatural influences. In order to some extent to understand their uneasiness and their astonishment, we need only read—to quote but one
instance among a thousand—a disquieting
but unassailable article, entitled, *Dans les
régions inexplorées de la biologie humaine.
Observations et expériences sur Eusapia
Paladino,* by Professor Bottazzi, Director
of the Physiological Institute of the University of Naples.[1] Seldom have experi-

[1] *Annales des sciences psychiques:* April-November
1907.

ments in the domain of mediums or spirits been conducted with more distrustful suspicion or with more implacable scientific strictness. Nevertheless, scattered limbs, pale, diaphanous but capable hands, suddenly appeared in the little physiological laboratory of Naples University, with its doors heavily padlocked and sealed, as it were, mathematically excluding any possibility of fraud; these same hands worked apparatus specially intended to register their touches; lastly, the outline of something black, of a head, uprose between the curtains of the mediumistic cabinet, remained visible for several seconds and did not retire until itself apparently frightened by the exclamations of surprise drawn from a group of scientists who, after all, were prepared for anything; and Professor Bottazzi confesses that it was then that, to quote his own words—measured words, as beseems a votary of science, but expressive—he felt "a shiver all through his body."

It was one of those moments in which a doubt which one had thought for ever abolished grips the most unbelieving. For the first time, perhaps, he looked around him with uncertainty and wondered in what world he was. As for the faithful adherents of the unknown, who had long understood that we must resign ourselves to understanding nothing and be prepared for every sort of surprise, there was here, all the same, even for them, a mystery of another character, a bewildering mystery, the only really strange mystery, more torturing than all the others together, because it verges upon ancestral fears and touches the most sensitive point of our destiny.

4

The spiritualistic argument most worthy of attention is that supplied by the appari-

tions of the dead and by haunted houses.
We will take no account of the phantasms
that precede, accompany or follow hard
upon death: they are explained by the
transmission of a violent emotion from one
subconsciousness to another; and, even
when they are not manifested until several
days after death, it may still be contended
that they are delayed telepathic communications. But what are we to say of the
ghosts that spring up more than a year,
nay, more than ten years after the disappearance of the corpse? They are very
rare, I know, but after all there are some
that are extremely difficult to deny, for the
accounts of their actions are attested and
corroborated by numerous and trustworthy
witnesses. It is true that here again,
where it is in most cases a question of apparitions to relations or friends, we may be
told that we are in the presence of telepathic incidents or of hallucinations of the

memory. We thus deprive the spiritualists of a new and considerable province of their realm. Nevertheless, they retain certain private demesnes into which our telepathic explanations do not penetrate so easily. There have in fact been ghosts that showed themselves to people who had never known or seen them in the flesh. They are more or less closely connected with the ghosts in haunted houses, to which we must revert for a moment.

As I said above, it is almost impossible honestly to deny the existence of these houses. Here again the telepathic interpretation enforces itself in the majority of cases. We may even allow it a strange but justifiable extension, for its limits are scarcely known. It has happened fairly often, for instance, that ghosts come to disturb a dwelling whose occupiers find, in response to their indications, bones hidden in the walls or under the floors. It is even possible, as in the case of William Moir,[1] which was as strictly conducted and supervised as a judicial enquiry, that the skeleton is buried at some distance from the house and dates more than forty years back. When the remains are removed and decently interred, the apparitions cease.

But even in the case of William Moir there is no sufficient reason for abandoning the telepathic theory. The medium, the "sensitive," as the English say, feels the presence or the proximity of the bones; some relation established between them and him—a relation which certainly is profoundly mysterious—makes him experience the last emotion of the deceased and sometimes allows him to conjure up the picture and the circumstances of the suicide or murder, even as, in telepathy between living persons, the contact of an inanimate object is able to bring him into direct rela-

[1] *Proceedings,* vol. vi., pp. 35-41.

tion with the subconsciousness of its owner. The slender chain connecting life and death is not yet entirely broken; and we might even go so far as to say that everything is still happening within our world.

But are there cases in which every link, however thin, however subtle we may deem it, is definitely shattered? Who would venture to maintain this? We are only beginning to suspect the elasticity, the flexibility, the complexity of those invisible threads which bind together objects, thoughts, lives, emotions, all that is on this earth and even that which does not yet exist to that which exists no longer. Let us take an instance in the first volume of the *Proceedings:* Mr. X. Z., who was known to most of the members of the Committee on Haunted Houses, and whose evidence was above suspicion, went to reside in a large old house, part of which was occupied by his friend Mr. G——. Mr.

The Unknown Guest

X. Z. knew nothing of the history of the
place except that two servants of Mr. G—'s
had given him notice on account of strange
noises which they had heard. One night—
it was the 22nd of September—Mr. X. Z.,
on his way up to his bedroom in the dark,
saw the whole passage filled with a dazzling
and uncanny light, and in this strange light
he saw the figure of an old man in a flow-
ered dressing-gown. As he looked, both
figure and light vanished and he was left
in pitch darkness. The next day, remembering the tales told by the two servants,
he made enquiries in the village. At first
he could find out nothing, but finally an old
lawyer told him that he had heard that the
grandfather of the present owner of the
house had strangled his wife and then cut
his own throat on the very spot where Mr.
X. Z. had seen the apparition. He was
unable to give the exact date of this double
event; but Mr. X. Z. consulted the parish

register and found that it had taken place on a 22nd of September.

On the 22nd of September of the following year, a friend of Mr. G—'s arrived to make a short stay. The morning after his arrival, he came down, pale and tired, and announced his intention of leaving immediately. On being questioned, he confessed that he was afraid, that he had been kept awake all night by the sound of groans, blasphemous oaths and cries of despair, that his bedroom door had been opened, and so forth.

Three years afterwards, Mr. X. Z. had occasion to call on the landlord of the house, who lived in London, and saw over the mantelpiece a picture which bore a striking resemblance to the figure which he had seen in the passage. He pointed it out to his friend Mr. G—, saying:

"That is the man whom I saw."

The landlord, in reply to their questions,

said that the painting was a portrait of his grandfather, adding that he had been "no credit to the family."

Evidently, this does not in any way prove the existence of ghosts or the survival of man. It is quite possible that, in spite of Mr. X. Z.'s undoubted good faith, imagination played a subtle but powerful part in these marvels. Perhaps it was set going by the stories of the two servants, insignificant gossip to which no attention was paid at the time, but which probably found its way down into the weird and fertile depths of the subconsciousness. The image was next transmitted by suggestion to the visitor frightened by a sleepless night. As for the recognition of the portrait, this is either the weakest or the most impressive part of the story, according to the theory that is being defended.

It is none the less certain that there is some unfairness in suggesting this explana-

45

tion for every incident of the kind. It means stretching to the uttermost and perhaps stretching too far the elastic powers of that amiable maid-of-all-work, telepathy. For that matter, there are cases in which the telepathic interpretation is even more uncertain, as in that described by Miss R. C. Morton in vol. viii. of the *Proceedings*.

The story is too long and complicated to be reproduced here. It is unnecessary to observe that, in view of the character of Miss Morton, a lady of scientific training, and of the quality of the corroborative testimony, the facts themselves seem incontestable.

The case is that of a house built in 1860, whose first occupier was an Anglo-Indian, the next tenant being an old man and the house then remaining unlet for four years. In 1882, when Captain Morton and his family moved in, there had never, so far as they knew, been any question of its being haunted. Three months afterwards, Miss Morton was in her room and on the point of getting into bed, when she heard some one at the door and went to it, thinking that it might be her mother. On opening the door, she found no one there, but, going a few steps along the passage, she saw a tall lady, dressed in black, standing at the head of the stairs. She did not wish to make the others uneasy and mentioned the occurrence to no one except a friend, who did not live in the neighbourhood.

But soon the same figure dressed in black was seen by the various members of the household, by a married sister on a visit to the house, by the father, by the other sisters, by a little boy, by a neighbour, General A——, who saw a lady crying in the orchard and, thinking that one of the daughters of the house was ill, sent to enquire after her. Even the Mortons' two dogs on more than one occasion clearly showed that they saw the phantom.

It was, as a matter of fact, very harmless: it said nothing; it wanted nothing; it wandered from room to room, without any apparent object; and, when it was spoken to, it did not answer and only made its escape. The household became accustomed to the apparition; it troubled nobody and inspired no terror. It was immaterial, it could not be touched, but yet it intercepted the light. After making enquiries, they succeeded in identifying it as the second wife of the Anglo-Indian. The Morton family had never seen the lady, but, from the description which they gave of the phantom to those who had known her, it appeared that the likeness was unmistakable. For the rest, they did not know why she came back to haunt a house in which she had not died. After 1887, the appearances became less frequent, distinct, ceasing altogether in 1889.

Let us assume that the facts as reported in the *Proceedings* are certain and indisputable. We have very nearly the ideal case, free from previous or ambient suggestion. If we refuse to believe in the existence of ghosts, if we are absolutely positive that the dead do not survive their death, then we must admit that the hallucination took birth spontaneously in the imagination of Miss Morton, an unconscious medium, and was subsequently transmitted by telepathy to all those around her. In my opinion, this explanation, however arbitrary and severe it may be, is the one which it behoves us to accept, pending further proofs. But it must be confessed that, in thus extending our incredulity, we render it very difficult for the dead to make their existence known.

We possess a certain number of cases of this kind, rigorously investigated, cases probably representing but an infinitesimal part of those which might be collected. Is it possible that they one and all elude the telepathic explanation? It would be necessary to make a study of them, conducted with the most scrupulous and unremitting attention; for the question is not devoid of interest. If the existence of ghosts were well-established, it would mean the entrance into this world, which we believe to be our world, of a new force that would explain more than one thing which we are still far from understanding. If the dead interfere at one point, there is no reason why they should not interfere at every other point. We should no longer be alone, among ourselves, in our hermetically-closed sphere, as we are perhaps only too ready to imagine it. We should have to alter more than one of our physical and moral laws, more than one of our ideas; and it would no doubt be the most important and the most

extraordinary revelation that would be expected in the present state of our knowledge and since the disappearance of the
old positive religions. But we are not
there yet: the proof of all this is still in
the nursery-stage; and I do not know if
it will ever get beyond that. Nevertheless
the fact remains that, in these impenetrable
regions of mystery which we are now ex-
ploring, the one weak spot lies here, the
one wall in which there seems to be a chink
—a strange one enough—giving a glimpse
into the other world. It is narrow and
vague and behind it there is still darkness;
but it is not without significance and we
shall do well not to lose sight of it.

6

Let us observe that this survival of the
dead, as the neospiritualists conceive it,
seems much less improbable since we have
been studying more closely the manifesta-

tions of the extraordinary and incontestable spiritual force that lies hidden within ourselves. It is not dependent on our thought, nor on our consciousness, nor on our will; and very possibly it is not dependent either on our life. While we are still breathing on this earth, it is already surmounting most of the great obstacles that limit and paralyse our existence. It acts at a distance and so to speak without organs. It passes through matter, disaggregates it and reconstitutes it. It seems to possess the gift of ubiquity. It is not subject to the laws of gravity and lifts weights out of all proportion with the real and measurable strength of the body whence it is believed to emanate. It releases and removes itself from that body; it comes and goes freely and takes to itself substances and shapes which it borrows all around it; and therefore it is no longer so strange to see it surviving for a time that body to which it does not appear to be as indissolubly bound as is our conscious existence. Is it necessary to add that this survival of a part of ourselves which we hardly know and which besides seems incomplete, incoherent and ephemeral is wholly without prejudice to our fate in the eternity of the worlds? But this is a question which we are not called upon to study here.

I shall perhaps be asked:

"If it is becoming increasingly difficult for all these facts—and there are more of them accumulating every day—to be embraced in the telepathic or psychometric theory, why not frankly accept the spiritualistic explanation, which is the simplest, which has an answer for everything and which is gradually encroaching on all the others?"

That is true: it is the simplest theory, perhaps too simple; and, like the religious theory, it dispenses us from all effort or seeking. We have nothing to set against it but the mediumistic theory, which doubtless does not account exactly for a good many things, but which at least is on the same side of the hill of life as ourselves and remains among us, upon our earth, within reach of our eyes, our hands, our thoughts and our researches. There was a time when lightning, epidemics and earthquakes were attributed without distinction to the wrath of Heaven. Nowadays, when we are more or less familiar with the source of the great infectious diseases, the hand of Providence knows them no more; and, though we are still ignorant of the nature of electricity and the laws that regulate seismic shocks, we no longer dream, while waiting to learn more about them, of looking for their causes in the judgment or anger of an imaginary Being. Let us act likewise in the present case. It behoves us above all to avoid those rash explanations which, in their haste, leave by the roadside a host of things that appear to be unknown or unknowable only because the necessary effort has not yet been made to know them. After all, while we must not eliminate the spiritualistic theory, neither must we content ourselves with it. It is even preferable not to linger over it until it has supplied us with decisive arguments, for it is the duty of this theory which sweeps us roughly out of our sphere to furnish us with such arguments. For the present, it simply relegates to posthumous regions phenomena that appear to occur within ourselves; it adds superfluous mystery and needless difficulty to the mediumistic mystery whence it springs. If we were concerned with facts that had no footing in this world, we should certainly have to turn our eyes in another direction; but we see a large number of actions performed which are of the same nature as those attributed

to the spirits and equally inexplicable, actions with which, however, we know that
they have nothing to do. When it is
proved that the dead exercise some intervention, we will bow before the fact as will-
ingly as we bow before the mediumistic
mysteries: it is a question of order, of in-
ternal policy and of scientific method much
more than of probability, preference or
fear. The hour has not yet come to abandon the principle which I have formulated
elsewhere with respect to our communications with the dead, namely, that it is natural that we should remain at home, in our
own world, as long as we can, as long as
we are not violently driven from it by a
series of irresistible and incontrovertible
proofs coming from the neighbouring abyss.
The survival of a spirit is no more improbable than the prodigious faculties which we
are obliged to attribute to the mediums if
we deny them to the dead. But the exist-

ence of mediums is beyond dispute, whereas that of spirits is not; and it is therefore for the spirits or for those who make use of their name to begin by proving that they exist. Before turning towards the mystery beyond the grave, let us first exhaust the possibilities of the mystery here on earth.

CHAPTER II

PSYCHOMETRY

CHAPTER II

PSYCHOMETRY

I

NOW that we have eliminated the gods and the dead, what have we left? Ourselves and all the life around us; and that is perhaps enough. It is, at any rate, much more than we are able to grasp.

Let us now study certain manifestations that are absolutely similar to those which we attribute to the spirits and quite as surprising. As for these manifestations, there is not the least doubt of their origin. They do not come from the other world; they are born and die upon this earth; and they arise solely and incontestably from our own actual living mystery. They are, moreover, of all psychic manifestations, those which are easiest to examine and verify, seeing that they can be repeated almost indefinitely and that a number of excellent and well-known mediums are always ready to reproduce them in the presence of any one interested in the question. It is no longer a case of uncertain and casual observation, but of scientific experiment.

The manifestations in question are so many phenomena of intuition, of clairvoyance or clairaudience, of seeing at a distance and even of seeing the future. These phenomena may either be due to pure, spontaneous intuition on the part of the medium, in an hypnotic or waking state, or else produced or facilitated by one of the various empirical methods which apparently serve only to arouse the medium's subconscious faculties and to release in some way his subliminal clairvoyance. Among such methods, those most often employed are, as we all know, cards, coffee-grounds, pins, the lines of the hand, crystal globes, astrology, and so on. They possess no importance in themselves, no intrinsic virtue, and are worth exactly what the medium who uses them is worth. As M. Duchatel well says:

"In reality, there is only one solitary *mancy*. The faculty of seeing in *time*, like the faculty of seeing in *space*, is *one*, whatever its outward form or the process employed."

We will not linger now over those manifestations which, under appearances that are sometimes childish and vulgar, often conceal surprising and incontestable truths, but will devote the present chapter exclusively to a series of phenomena which includes almost all the others and which has been classed under the generic and rather ill-chosen and ill-constructed title of "psychometry." Psychometry, to borrow Dr. Maxwell's excellent definition, is "the faculty possessed by certain persons of placing themselves in relation, either spontaneously or, for the most part, through the intermediary of some object, with unknown and often very distant things and people."

The existence of this faculty is no longer seriously denied; and it is easy for any one who cares to do so to verify it for himself; for the mediums who possess it are not extremely rare, nor are they inaccessible. It has formed the subject of a number of experiments (see, among others, M. Warcollier's report in the *Annales des sciences psychiques* of July, 1911) and of a few treatises, in the front rank of which I would mention M. Duchatel's *Enquête sur des cas de psychométrie* and Dr. Osty's recently published book, *Lucidité et intuition*, which is the fullest, most profound and most conscientious work that we possess on the matter up to the present. Nevertheless it may be said that these regions quite lately annexed by metapsychical science are as yet hardly explored and that fruitful surprises are doubtless awaiting earnest seekers.

2

The faculty in question is one of the strangest faculties of our subconsciousness and beyond a doubt contains the key to most of the manifestations that seem to proceed from another world. Let us begin by seeing, with the aid of a living and typical example, how it is exercised.

Mme. M——, one of the best mediums mentioned by Dr. Osty, is given an object which belonged to or which has been touched and handled by a person about whom it is proposed to question her. Mme. M—— operates in a state of trance; but there are other noted psychometers, such as Mme. F—— and M. Ph. M. de F——, who retain all their normal consciousness, so that hypnotism or the somnambulistic state is in no way indispensable to the awakening of this extraordinary faculty of clairvoyance.

When the object, which is usually a letter, has been handed to Mme. M——, she is asked to place herself in communication with the writer of the letter or the owner of the object. Forthwith, Mme. M—— not only sees the person in question, his physical appearance, his character, his habits, his interests, his state of health, but also, in a series of rapid and changing visions that follow upon one another like cinematograph pictures, perceives and describes exactly his immediate surroundings, the scenery outside his window, the rooms in which he lives, the people who live with him and who wish him well or ill, the psychology and the most secret and unexpected intentions of all those who figure in his existence. If, by means of your questions, you direct her towards the past, she traces the whole course of the subject's history. If you turn her towards the future, she seems often to discover it as clearly as the past. But we will for the moment reserve this latter point, to which we shall return later in a chapter devoted to the knowledge of the future.

3

In the presence of these phenomena, the first thought that naturally occurs to the mind is that we are once more concerned with that astonishing and involuntary communication between one subconsciousness and another which has been invested with the name of telepathy. And there is no denying that telepathy plays a great part in these intuitions. However, to explain their working, nothing is equal to an example based upon a personal experience. Here is one which is in no way remarkable, but which plainly shows the normal course of the operation.

The Unknown Guest

In September, 1913, while I was at Elberfeld, visiting Krall's horses, my wife went to consult Mme. M——, gave her a scrap of writing in my hand—a note dispatched previous to my journey and containing no allusion to it—and asked her where I was and what I was doing. Without a second's hesitation, Mme. M—— declared that I was very far away, in a foreign country where they spoke a language which she did not understand. She saw first a paved yard, shaded by a big tree, with a building on the left and a garden at the back: a rough but not inapt description of Krall's stables, which my wife did not know and which I myself had not seen at the time when I wrote the note. She next perceived me in the midst of the horses, examining them, studying them with an absorbed, anxious and tired air. This was true, for I found those visits, which overwhelmed me with a sense of the marvellous and kept my attention on the rack, singularly exhausting and bewildering. My wife asked her if I intended to buy the horses. She replied:

"Not at all; he is not thinking of it."

And, seeking her words as though to express an unaccustomed and obscure thought, she added:

"I don't know why he is so much interested; it is not like him. He has no particular passion for horses. He has some lofty idea which I can't quite discover. . . ."

She made two rather curious mistakes in this experiment. The first was that, at the time when she saw me in Krall's stable-yard, I was no longer there. She had received her vision just in the interval of a few hours between two visits. Experience shows, however, that this is a usual error among psychometers. They do not, properly speaking, see the action at the very mo-

ment of its performance, but rather the
customary and familiar action, the principal thing that preoccupies either the person
about whom they are being consulted or the
person consulting them. They frequently
go astray in time. There is not, therefore,
necessarily any simultaneity between the action and the vision; and it is well never to
take their statements in this respect literally.

The other mistake referred to our dress:
Krall and I were in ordinary town clothes,
whereas she saw us in those long coats
which stable-lads wear when grooming their
horses.

Let us now make every allowance for my
wife's unconscious suggestions: she knew
that I was at Elberfeld and that I should
be in the midst of the horses; and she knew
or could easily conjecture my state of mind.
The transmission of thought is remarkable;
but this is a recognized phenomenon and

one of frequent occurrence and we need not therefore linger over it.

The real mystery begins with the description of a place which my wife had never seen and which I had not seen either at the time of writing the note which established the psychometrical communication. Are we to believe that the appearance of what I was one day to see was already inscribed on that prophetic sheet of paper, or more simply and more probably that the paper which represented myself was enough to transmit either to my wife's subconsciousness or to Mme. M——, whom at that time I had never met, an exact picture of what my eyes beheld three or four hundred miles away? But, although this description is exceedingly accurate—paved yard, big tree, building on the left, garden at the back—is it not too general for all idea of chance coincidence to be eliminated? Perhaps, by insisting further, greater precision

71

might have been obtained; but this is not certain, for as a rule the pictures follow upon one another so swiftly in the medium's vision that he has no time to perceive the details. When all is said, experiences of this kind do not enable us to go beyond the telepathic explanation. But here is a different one, in which subconscious suggestion cannot play any part whatever.

Some days after the experiment which I have related, I received from England a request for my autograph. Unlike most of those which assail an author of any celebrity, it was charming and unaffected; but it told me nothing about its writer. Without even noticing from what town it was sent to me, after showing it to my wife, I replaced it in its envelope and took it to Mme. M——. She began by describing us, my wife and myself, who both of us had touched the paper and consequently impregnated it with our respective "fluids."

The Unknown Guest

I asked her to pass beyond us and come to the writer of the note. She then saw a girl of fifteen or sixteen, almost a child, who had been in rather indifferent health, but who was now very well indeed. The girl was in a beautiful garden, in front of a large and luxurious house standing in the midst of rather hilly country. She was playing with a big, curly-haired, long-eared dog. Through the branches of the trees one caught a glimpse of the sea.

On enquiry, all the details were found to be astonishingly accurate; but, as usual, there was a mistake in the time, that is to say, the girl and her dog were not in the garden at the instant when the medium saw them there. Here again an habitual action had obscured a casual movement; for, as I have already said, the vision very rarely corresponds with the momentary reality.

4

There is nothing exceptional in the above example; I selected it from among many others because it is simple and clear. Besides, this kind of experience is already, so to speak, classical, or at least should be so, were it not that everything relating to the manifestations of our subconsciousness is always received with extraordinary suspicion. In any case, I cannot too often repeat that the experiment is within everybody's reach; and it rarely fails to achieve absolute success with capable psychometers, who are pretty well known and whom it is open to any one to consult.

Let us add that it can be extended much further. If, for instance, I had acted as I did in similar cases and asked the medium questions about the young girl's home-circle, about the character of her father, the health of her mother, the tastes and habits of her brothers and sisters, she would have

74

answered with the same certainty, the same
precision as one might do who was not only
a close acquaintance of the girl's, but endowed with much more penetrating faculties of intuition than a normal observer. In
short, she would have felt and expressed all
that this girl's subconsciousness would have
felt with regard to the persons mentioned.
But it must be admitted that, as we are
here no longer speaking of facts that are
easily verified, confirmation becomes infinitely more difficult.

There could be no question, in the circumstances, of transmission of thought,
since both the medium and I were ignorant
of everything. Besides, other experiments,
easily devised and repeated and more rigorously controlled, do away with that theory
entirely. For instance, I took three letters
written by intimate friends, put each of
them in a double envelope and gave them
to a messenger unacquainted with the con-

tents of the envelopes and also with the persons in question to take to Mme. M——. On arriving at the house, the messenger handed the clairvoyant one of the letters, selected at random, and did nothing further beyond putting the indispensable questions, likewise at random, and taking down the medium's replies in shorthand. Mme. M—— began by giving a very striking physical portrait of the lady who had written the letter; followed this up with an absolutely faithful description of her character, her habits, her tastes, her intellectual and moral qualities; and ended by adding a few details concerning her private life, of which I myself was entirely unaware and of which I obtained the confirmation shortly afterwards. The experiment yielded just as remarkable results when continued with the two other letters.

In the face of this mystery, two explanations may be offered, both equally perplexing. On the one hand, we shall have to admit that the sheet of paper handed to the psychometer and impregnated with human "fluid" contains, after the manner of some prodigiously compressed gas, all the incessantly renewed, incessantly recurring images that surround a person, all his past and perhaps his future, his psychology, his state of health, his wishes, his intentions, often unknown to himself, his most secret instincts, his likes and dislikes, all that is bathed in light and all that is plunged in darkness, his whole life, in short, and more than his personal and conscious life, besides all the lives and all the influences, good or bad, latent or manifest, of all who approach him. We should have here a mystery as unfathomable and at least as vast as that of generation, which transmits, in an infinitesimal particle, the mind and matter, with all the qualities and all the faults, all the acquirements and all the history, of a series of lives of which none can tell the number.

On the other hand, if we do not admit that so much energy can lie concealed in a sheet of paper, continuing to exist and develop indefinitely there, we must necessarily suppose that an inconceivable network of nameless forces is perpetually radiating from this same paper, forces which, cleaving time and space, detect instantaneously, anywhere and at any distance, the life that gave them life and place themselves in complete communication, body and soul, senses and thoughts, past and future, consciousness and subconsciousness, with an existence lost amid the innumerous host of men who people this earth. It is, indeed, exactly what happens in the experiments with mediums in automatic speech or writing, who believe themselves to be inspired by the dead. Yet, here it is no longer a discarnate spirit, but an object of any kind imbued with a living "fluid" that works the miracle; and this, we may remark in passing, deals a severe blow to the spiritualistic theory.

Nevertheless, there are two rather serious objections to this second explanation. Granting that the object really places the medium in communication with an unknown entity discovered in space, how comes it that the image or the spectacle created by that communication hardly ever corresponds with the reality at the actual moment? On the other hand, it is indisputable that the psychometer's clairvoyance, his gift of seeing at a distance the pictures and scenes surrounding an unknown being, is exercised with the same certainty and the same power when the object that sets his strange faculty at work has been touched by a person who has been dead for years. Are we, then, to admit that there is an actual, living communication with a human being who is no more, who sometimes—as, for instance, in a case of incineration—has left no trace of himself on earth, in short, with a dead man who continues to live at the place and at the moment at which he impregnated the object with his "fluid" and who seems to be unaware that he is dead?

But these objections are perhaps less serious than one might believe. To begin with, there are seers, so-called "tele-psychics," who are not psychometers, that is to say, they are able to communicate with an unknown and distant person without the intermediary of an object; and in these seers, as in the psychometers, the vision very rarely corresponds with the actual facts of the moment: they too perceive above all the general impression, the usual and characteristic actions. Next, as regards communications with a person long since dead, we are confronted with one of two things: either confirmation will be almost impossible when it concerns revelations on the subject of the dead man's private deeds and actions, which are unknown to any living person; or else communication will be established not with the deceased, but with the living person, who necessarily knows the facts which he is called upon to confirm. As Dr. Osty very rightly says:

"The conditions are then those of perception by the intermediary of the thoughts of a living person; and the deceased is perceived through a mental representation. The experiment, for this reason, is valueless as evidence of the reality of retrospective psychometry and consequently of the recording part played by the object.

"The only class of experiment that could be of value from this point of view, would be that in which confirmation would come subsequently from documents whose contents remained unknown to any living person until after the clairvoyance sitting. It might then be proved that the object can latently register the human personalities which have touched it and that it is sufficient in itself to allow of a mental reconstruction of those personalities through the interpretation of the register by a clairvoyant or psychometer."

5

It may be imagined that experiments of this sort, in which there is no crack, no leak on the side of the living, are anything but easy to carry through. In the case of a murder, for instance, it can always be maintained that the medium discovers the body and the circumstances of the tragedy through the involuntary and unconscious intermediary of the murderer, even when the latter escapes prosecution and suspicion altogether. But a recent incident, related by Dr. Osty with the utmost precision of detail and the most scrupulous verification in the *Annales des sciences psychiques* of April, 1914, perhaps supplies us with one of those experiments which we have not been able to achieve until this day. I give the facts in a few words.

On the 2nd of Mach of this year, M. Étienne Lerasle, an old man of eighty-two, left his son's house at Cours-les-Barres (Cher) for his daily walk and was not seen again. The house stands in the middle of a forest on Baron Jaubert's estate. Vain searches were made in every direction for the missing man's traces; the ponds and pools were dragged to no purpose; and on the 8th of March a careful and systematical exploration of the wood, in which no fewer than twenty-four people took part, led to no result. At last, on the 18th of March, M. Louis Mirault, Baron Jaubert's agent, thought of applying to Dr. Osty, and supplied him with a scarf which the old man had worn. Dr. Osty went to his favourite medium, Mme. M——. He knew only one thing, that the matter concerned an old man of eighty-two, who walked with a slight stoop; and that was all.

As soon as Mme. M—— had taken the scarf in her hands, she saw the dead body of an old man lying on the damp ground, in a wood, in the middle of a coppice, beside a horse-shoe pond, near a sort of rock. She traced the road taken by the victim, depicted the buildings which he had passed, his mental condition impaired by age, his fixed intention of dying, his physical appearance, his habitual and characteristic way of carrying his stick, his soft striped shirt, and so on.

The accuracy of the description caused the greatest astonishment among the missing man's friends. There was one detail that puzzled them a little: the mention of a rock in a part of the country that possessed none. The search was resumed on the strength of the data supplied by the clairvoyant. But all the roads in a forest are more or less alike; the indications were not enough; and nothing was found.

It so happened that the second and third interviews with Mme. M—— had to be postponed until the 30th of March and the 6th of April following. At each of these sittings, the details of the vision and of the road taken became clearer and clearer and were given with startling precision, so much so that, by pursuing step by step the indications of the medium, the man's friends ended by discovering the body, dressed as stated, lying in the middle of a coppice, just as described, close to a huge stump of a tree all covered with moss, which might easily be mistaken for a rock, and on the edge of a crescent-shaped piece of water.

I may add that these particular indications applied to no other part of the wood.

6

I refer the reader to Dr. Osty's conscientious and exhaustive article for the numerous details which I have been obliged to omit; but those which I have given are enough to show the character of this extraordinary case. To begin with, we have one certainty which appears almost unassailable, namely, that there can be no question of a crime. No one had the least interest in procuring the old man's death. The body bore no marks of violence; besides, the minds of those concerned did not for a moment entertain the thought of an assault. The poor man, whose mental derangement was known to all those about him, obsessed by the desire and thought of death, had gone quietly and obstinately to seek it in the nearest coppice. There was therefore no criminal in the case, in other words, there was no possible or imaginable communication between the medium's subconsciousness and that of any living person. Hence we are compelled to admit that the communication was established with the dead man or with his subconsciousness, which continued to live for nearly a month after his death and to wander around the same places; or else we must agree that all this coming tragedy, all that the old man was about to see, do and suffer was already irrevocably contained and inscribed in the scarf at the moment when he last wore it.

In this particular case, considering that all relations with the living were definitely and undeniably severed, I can see no other explanations beyond these two. They are both equally astounding and land us suddenly in a world of fable and enchantment which we thought that we had left for good and all. If we do not adopt the theory

of the tell-tale scarf, we must accept that
of the spiritualists, who maintain that the
spirits communicate with us freely. It is
possible that they may find a serious argument in this case. But a solitary fact is not
enough to support a theory, all the more
so as the one in question will never be absolutely safe from the objection that could be
raised if the case were one of murder, which
is possible, after all, and cannot be actually
disproved. We must, therefore, while
awaiting other similar and more decisive
facts, if any such are conceivable, return
to those which are, so to speak, laboratory
facts, facts which are only denied by those
who will not take the trouble to verify
them; and to interpret these facts there are
only the two theories which we mentioned
above, before this digression; for, in these
cases, which are unlike those of automatic
speech or writing, we have not as a rule to
consider the possibility of any intervention

of the dead. As a matter of fact, the best-known psychometers are very rarely spiritualists and claim no connection with the spirits. They care but little, as a rule, about the source of their intuitions and seem very little interested in their exact workng and origin. Now it would be exceedingly surprising if, acting and speaking in the name of the departed, they should be so consistently ignorant of the existence of those who inspire them; and more surprising still if the dead, whom in other circumstances we see so jealously vindicating their identity, should not here, when the occasion is so propitious, seek to declare themselves, to manifest themselves and to make themselves known.

7

Dismissing for the time being the intervention of the dead, I believe then that, in most of the cases which I will call laboratory cases, because they can be reproduced at will, we are not necessarily reduced to the theory of the vitalized object representing wholly, indefinitely and inexhaustibly, through all the vicissitudes of time and space, every one of those who have held it in their hands for a little while. For we must not forget that, according to this theory, the object in question will conceal and, through the intermediary of the medium, will reveal as many distinct and complete personalities as it has undergone contacts. It will never confuse or mix those different personalities. They will remain there in definite strata, distinct one from another; and, as Dr. Osty puts it, "the medium can interpret each of them from beginning to end, as though he were in communication with the far-off entity."

All this makes the theory somewhat incredible, even though it be not much more so than the many other phenomena in which the shock of the miraculous has been softened by familiarity. We can find more or less everywhere in nature that prodigious faculty of storing away inexhaustible energies and ineffaceable traces, memories and impressions in space. There is not a thing in this world that is lost, that disappears, that ceases to be, to retain and to propagate life. Need we recall, in this connection, the incessant emission of pictures perceived by the sensitized plate, the vibrations of sound that accumulate in the disks of the gramophone, the Hertzian waves that lose none of their strength in space, the mysteries of reproduction and, in a word, the incomprehensibility of everything around us?

8

Personally, if I had to choose, I should, in most of these laboratory cases, frankly adopt the theory that the object touched serves simply to detect, among the prodigious crowd of human beings, the one who impregnated it with his "fluid."

"This object," says Dr. Osty, "has no other function than to allow the medium's sensitiveness to distinguish a definite force from among the innumerable forces that assail it."

It seems more and more certain that, as the cells of an immense organism, we are connected with everything that exists by an inextricable network of vibrations, waves, influences, of nameless, numberless and uninterrupted fluids. Nearly always, in nearly all men, everything carried along by these invisible wires falls into the depths of the unconsciousness and passes unperceived, which does not mean that it remains inactive. But sometimes an exceptional circumstance—in the present case, the marvellous sensibility of a first-class medium—

suddenly reveals to us, by the vibrations and the undeniable action of one of those wires, the existence of the infinite network. I will not speak here of trails discovered and followed in an almost mediumistic manner, after an object of some sort has been sniffed at. Such stories, though highly probable, as yet lack adequate support. But, within a similar order of ideas, and in a humbler world and one with more modest limits, the dog, for instance, is incessantly surrounded by different scents and smells to which he appears indifferent until his attention is aroused by one or other of these vagrant effluvia, when he extricates it from the hopeless tangle. It would seem as though the trail took life, vibrating like a chord in unison with the animal's wishes, becoming irresistible, and taking it to its goal after innumerable winds and turns.

We see the mysterious network revealed also in "cross-correspondence." Two or three mediums who do not know one another, who are often separated by seas or continents, who are ignorant of the whereabouts of the one who is to complete their thought, each write a part of a sentence which, as it stands, conveys no meaning whatever. On piecing the fragments together, we perceive that they fit to perfection and acquire an intelligible and obviously premeditated sense. We here find once more the same faculty that permits the medium to detect, among thousands of others, a definite force which was wandering in space. It is true that, in these cases, the spiritualists maintain that the whole experiment is organized and directed by a discarnate intelligence, independent of the mediums, which means to prove its existence and its identity in this manner. Without incontinently rejecting this theory, which is not necessarily indefensible, we will merely remark that, since the faculty is manifested

in psychometry without the intervention of
the spirits, there can be no sufficient reason
for attributing it to them in cross-correspondence.

9

But in whom does it reside? Is it hidden in ourselves or in the medium? According to Dr. Osty, the clairvoyants are
mirrors reflecting the intuitive thought that
is latent in each of us. In other words, it
is we ourselves who are clairvoyant, and
they but reveal to us our own clairvoyance.
Their mission is to stir, to awaken, to gal-
vanize, to illumine the secrets of our subconsciousness and to bring them to the surface of our normal lives. They act upon
our inner darkness exactly as, in the photographic dark-room, the developing-bath
acts upon the sensitized plate. I am convinced that the theory is accurate as regards intuition and clairvoyance proper,

that is to say, in all cases where we are in the medium's presence and more or less directly in touch with him. But is it so in psychometry? Is it we who, unknown to ourselves, know all that the object contains, or is it the medium alone who discovers it in the object itself, independently of the person who produces the object? When, for instance, we receive a letter from a stranger, does this letter, which has absorbed like a sponge the whole life and by choice the subconscious life of the writer, disgorge all that it contained into our subconsciousness? Do we instantly learn all that concerns its author, absolutely as though he were standing before us in the flesh and, above all, with his soul laid bare, though we remain profoundly ignorant of the fact that we have learnt it until the medium's intervention tells us so?

This, if you like, is simply shifting the question. Let it be the medium or myself that discovers the unknown personality in the object or tracks it across time and space: all that we do is to widen the scope of our riddle, while leaving it no less obscure. Nevertheless, there is some interest in knowing whether we have to do with a general faculty latent in all men or an inexplicable privilege reserved to rare individuals. The exceptional should always be eliminated, if possible, and not left to hang over the abyss like an unfinished bridge leading to nothing. I am well aware that the compulsory intervention of the medium implies that, in spite of all, we recognize his possession of abnormal faculties; but at any rate we reduce their power and their extent appreciably and we return sooner and more easily to the ordinary laws of the great human mystery. And it is of importance that we should be ever coming back to that mystery and ever bringing all things back to it. But, unfortunately, actual experience does not admit of this generalization. It is clearly a case of a special faculty, one peculiar to the medium, one which is wholly unknown to our latent intuition. We can easily assure ourselves of this by causing the medium to receive through a third party and enclosed in a series of three envelopes, as in the experiment described above, a letter of which we know the writer, but of which both the source and the contents are absolutely unknown to the messenger. These unusual circumstances, in which all subconscious communications between consultant and consulted are strictly cut off, will in no way hamper the medium's clairvoyance; and we may fairly conclude that it is actually the medium himself who discovers directly, without an intermediary, without "relays," to use M. Duchatel's expression, all that the object holds concealed. It, therefore, seems certain that there is, at least in psychometry, something more than the mere mirror of which Dr. Osty speaks.

10

I consider it necessary to declare for the last time that these psychometric phenomena, astonishing though they appear at first, are known, proved and certain and are no longer denied or doubted by any of those who have studied them seriously. I could have given full particulars of a large number of conclusive experiments; but this seemed to me as superfluous and tedious as would be, for instance, a string of names of the recognized chemical reactions that can be obtained in a laboratory. Any one who pleases is at liberty to convince himself of the reality of the facts, provided that he applies to genuine mediums and keeps aloof from the inferior "seers" and especially the shams and imposters who swarm in this region more than in any other.

Even with the best of them, he will have
to be careful of the involuntary, unconscious and almost inevitable interference
of telepathy, which is also very interesting,
though it is a phenomenon of a different
class, much less surprising and debatable
than pure psychometry. He must also learn
the art of interrogating the medium and
refrain from asking incoherent and random
questions about casual or future events. He
will not forget that "clairvoyance is strictly
limited to the perception of human personality," according to the rule so well formulated by Dr. Osty. Experiments have been
made in which a psychometer, on touching
the tooth of a prehistoric animal, saw the
landscapes and the cataclysms of the
earth's earliest ages displayed before his
eyes; in which another medium, on handling
a jewel, conjured up, it would seem with
marvellous exactness, the games and pro-
cessions of ancient Greece, as though the

objects permanently retained the recollection or rediscovered the "astral negatives" of all the events which they once witnessed. But it will be understood that, in such cases, any effective control is, so to speak, impossible and that the part played by telepathy cannot be decided. It is important, therefore, to keep strictly to that which can be verified.

Even when thus limiting his scope, the experimenter will meet with many surprises. For instance, though the revelations of two psychometers to whom the same letter is handed in succession most often agree remarkably in their main outlines, it can also happen that one of them perceives only what concerns the writer of the letter, whereas the other will be interested only in the person to whom the letter was addressed or to a third person who was in the room where the letter was written. It is well to be forearmed against these first mistakes, which, for that matter, in the frequent cases where strict control is possible, but confirm the existence and the independence of the astounding faculty.

II

As for the theories that attempt to explain it, I am quite willing to grant that they are still somewhat confused. The important thing for the moment is the accumulation of cases and experiments that go feeling their way farther and farther along all the paths of the unknown. Meanwhile, than one unexpected door which sheds at the back of our old convictions more than one unexpected door, which sheds upon the life and habits of our secret being sufficient light to puzzle us for many a long day. This brings us back once more to the omniscience and perhaps the omnipotence of our hidden guest, to the brink of the mysterious reservoir of every manner of knowledge which we shall meet with again when we come to speak of the future, of the talking horses, of the divining-rod, of materializations and miracles, in short, in every circumstance where we pass beyond the horizon of our little daily life. As we thus advance, with slow and cautious foot-steps, in these as yet deserted and very nebulous regions of metapsychics, we are compelled to recognize that there must exist somewhere, in this world or in others, a spot in which everything is known, in which everything is possible, to which every-thing goes, from which everything comes, which belongs to all, to which all have access, but of which the long-forgotten roads must be learnt again by our stumbling feet. We shall often meet those difficult roads in the course of our present quest and we shall have more than one occasion to refer again to those depths into which all the supernatural facts of our existence flow, unless indeed they take their source there. For the moment, that which must above all engage our attention in these psychometric phenomena is their purely and exclusively human character. They occur between the living and the living, on this solid earth of ours, in the world that lies before our eyes; and the spirits, the dead, the gods and the interplanetary intelligences know them not. Hardly anywhere else, except in the equally perplexing manifestations of the divining-rod and in certain materializations, shall we find with the same clearness this same specific character, if one may call it so. This is a valuable lesson. It tells us that our every-day life provides phenomena as disturbing and of exactly the same kind and nature as those which, in other circumstances, we attribute to other forces than ours. It teaches us also that we must first direct and exhaust our enquiries here below, among ourselves, before passing to the other side; for our first care should be to simplify the interpretations and explanations and not to seek elsewhere, in suppositions, what probably lies hidden within us in reality. Afterwards, if the unknown overwhelm us utterly, if the darkness engulf us beyond all hope, there will still be time to go, none can tell where, to question the deities or the dead.

CHAPTER III

THE KNOWLEDGE OF THE FUTURE

CHAPTER III

THE KNOWLEDGE OF THE FUTURE

I

PREMONITION or precognition leads us to still more mysterious regions, where stands, half-emerging from an intolerable darkness, the gravest problem that can thrill mankind, the knowledge of the future. The latest, the best and the most complete study devoted to it is, I believe, that recently published by M. Ernest Bozzano, under the title *Des Phenomènes Prémonitoires*. Availing himself of excellent earlier work, notably that of Mrs. Sidgwick and Myers[1] and adding the result of his own researches, the author collects some thousand cases of precognition, of which he discusses one hundred and sixty, leaving the

[1] *Proceedings,* Vols. V. and XI.

great majority of the others on one side,
not because they are negligible, but because he does not wish to exceed too fla-
grantly the normal limits of a monograph.

He begins by carefully eliminating all
the episodes which, though apparently premonitory, may be explained by self-suggestion (as in the case, for instance, where
some one smitten with a disease still latent
seems to foresee this disease and the death
which will be its conclusion), by telepathy
(when a sensitive is aware beforehand of
the arrival of a person or a letter), or lastly
by clairvoyance (when a man dreams of a
spot where he will find something which
he has mislaid, or an uncommon plant, or
an insect sought for in vain, or of the unknown place which he will visit at some
later date).

In all these cases, we have not, properly
speaking, to do with a pure future, but
rather with a present that is not yet known.

Thus reduced and stripped of all foreign influences and intrusions, the number of instances in which there is a really clear and incontestable perception of a fragment of the future remains large enough, contrary to what is generally believed, to make it impossible for us to speak of extraordinary accidents or wonderful coincidences. There must be a limit to everything, even to distrust, even to the most extensive incredulity, otherwise all historical research and a good deal of scientific research would become decidedly impracticable. And this remark applies as much to the nature of the incidents related as to the actual authenticity of the narratives. We can contest or suspect any story whatever, any written proof, any evidence; but thenceforward we must abandon all certainty or knowledge that is not acquired by means of mathematical operations or laboratory experiments, that is to say, three-fourths of the human phenomena which interest us most. Observe that the records collected by the investigators of the S. P. R., like those discussed by M. Bozzano, are all told at first hand and that those stories of which the narrators were not the protagonists or the direct witnesses have been ruthlessly rejected. Furthermore, some of these narratives are necessarily of the nature of medical observations; as for the others, if we attentively examine the character of those who have related them and the circumstances which corroborate them, we shall agree that it is more just and more reasonable to believe in them than to look upon every man who has an extraordinary experience as being *a priori* a liar, the victim of an hallucination, or a wag.

2

There could be no question of giving

here even a brief analysis of the most striking cases. It would require a hundred
pages and would alter the whole nature of
this essay, which, to keep within its proper
dimensions, must take it for granted that
most of the materials which it examines
are familiar. I therefore refer the reader
who may wish to form an opinion for himself to the easily-accessible sources which I
have mentioned above. It will suffice, to
give an accurate idea of the gravity of the
problem to any one who has not time or
opportunity to consult the original documents if I sum up in a few words some of
these pioneer adventures, selected among
those which seem least open to dispute; for
it goes without saying that all have not the
same value, otherwise the question would be
settled. There are some which, while exceedingly striking at first sight and offer-
ing every guarantee that could be desired
as to authenticity, nevertheless do not imply

a real knowledge of the future and can be interpreted in another manner. I give one, to serve as an instance; it is reported by Dr. Alphonse Teste in his *Manuel pratique du magnétisme animal*.

On the 8th of May, Dr. Teste magnetizes Mme. Hortense ——————— in the presence of her husband. She is no sooner asleep than she announces that she has been pregnant for a fortnight, that she will not go her full time, that "she will take fright at something," that she will have a fall and that the result will be a miscarriage. She adds that, on the 12th of May, after having had a fright, she will have a fainting-fit which will last for eight minutes; and she then describes, hour by hour, the course of her malady, which will end in three days' loss of reason, from which she will recover.

On awaking, she retains no recollection of anything that has passed; it is kept from her; and Dr. Teste communicates his notes to Dr. Amédée Latour. On the 12th of May, he calls on M. and Mme. ————, finds them at table and puts Mme. ———— to sleep again, whereupon she repeats word for word what she told him four days before. They wake her up. The dangerous hour is drawing near. They take every imaginable precaution and even close the shutters. Mme. ————, made uneasy by these extraordinary measures which she is quite unable to understand, asks what they are going to do to her. Half-past three o'clock strikes. Mme. ———— rises from the sofa on which they have made her sit and wants to leave the room. The doctor and her husband try to prevent her.

"But what is the matter with you?" she asks. "I simply must go out."

"No, madame, you shall not: I speak in the interest of your health."

"Well, then, doctor," she replies, with

a smile, "if it is in the interest of my health, that is all the more reason why you should let me go out."

The excuse is a plausible one and even irresistible; but the husband, wishing to carry the struggle against destiny to the last, declares that he will accompany his wife. The doctor remains alone, feeling somewhat anxious, in spite of the rather farcical turn which the incident has taken. Suddenly, a piercing shriek is heard and the noise of a body falling. He runs out and finds Mme. ————— wild with fright and apparently dying in her husband's arms. At the moment when, leaving him for an instant, she opened the door of the place where she was going, a rat, the first seen there for twenty years, rushed at her and gave her so great a start that she fell flat on her back. And all the rest of the prediction was fulfilled to the letter, hour by hour and detail by detail.

3

To make it quite clear in what spirit I am undertaking this study and to remove at the beginning any suspicion of blind or systematic credulity, I am anxious, before going any further, to say that I fully realize that cases of this kind by no means carry conviction. It is quite possible that everything happened in the subconscious imagination of the subject and that she herself created, by self-suggestion, her illness, her fright, her fall and her miscarriage and adapted herself to most of the circumstances which she had foretold in her secondary state. The appearance of the rat at the fatal moment is the only thing that would suggest a precise and disquieting vision of an inevitable future event. Unfortunately, we are not told that the rat was perceived by other witnesses than the patient, so that there is nothing to prove that it also was not imaginary. I have therefore quoted this inadequate instance only because it represents fairly well the general aspect and the indecisive value of many similar cases and enables us to note once and for all the objections which can be raised and the precautions which we should take before entering these suspicious and obscure regions.

We now come to an infinitely more significant and less questionable case related by Dr. Joseph Maxwell, the learned and very scrupulous author of *Les Phénomènes psychiques,* a work which has been translated into English under the title of *Metapsychical Phenomena.* It concerns a vision which was described to him eight days before the event and which he told to many people before it was accomplished. A sensitive perceived in a crystal the following scene: a large steamer, flying a flag of three horizontal bars, black, white and red, and bearing the name *Leutschland,* was sailing in mid-ocean. The boat was suddenly enveloped in smoke; a great number of sailors, passengers and men in uniform rushed to the upper deck; and the boat went down.

Eight days afterwards, the newspapers announced the accident to the *Deutschland,* whose boiler had burst, obliging the steamboat to stand to.

The evidence of a man like Dr. Maxwell, especially when we have to do with a so-to-speak personal incident, possesses an importance on which it is needless to insist. We have here, therefore, several days beforehand, the very clear prevision of an event which, moreover, in no way concerns the percipient: a curious detail, but one which is not uncommon in these cases. The mistake in reading *Leutschland* for *Deutschland,* which would have been quite natural in real life, adds a note of probability and authenticity to the phenomenon.

As for the final act, the foundering of the vessel in the place of a simple heaving to, we must see in this, as Dr. J. W. Pickering and W. A. Sadgrove suggest, "the subconscious dramatization of a subliminal inference of the percipient." Such dramatizations, moreover, are instinctive and almost general in this class of visions.

If this were an isolated case, it would certainly not be right to attach decisive importance to it; "but," Dr. Maxwell observes, "the same sensitive has given me other curious instances; and these cases, compared with others which I myself have observed or with those of which I have received first-hand accounts, render the hypothesis of coincidence very improbable, though they do not absolutely exclude it."[1]

4

Another and perhaps more convincing case, more strictly investigated and estab-

[1]MAXWELL: *Metapsychical Phenomena*, p. 202.

lished, a case which clearly does not admit of explanation, by the theory of coincidence, worthy of all respect though this theory be, is that related by M. Théodore Flournoy, science professor at the university of Geneva, in his remarkable work, *Esprits et Médiums*. Professor Flournoy is known to be one of the most learned and most critical exponents of the new science of metapsychics. He even carries his fondness for natural explanations and his repugnance to admit the intervention of superhuman powers to a point where it is often difficult to follow him. I will give the narrative as briefly as possible. It will be found in full on pp. 348 to 362 of his masterly book.

In August, 1883, a certain Mme. Buscarlet, whom he knew personally, returned to Geneva after spending three years with the Moratief family at Kazan as governess to two girls. She continued to correspond with the family and also with a Mme. Nitchinof, who kept a school at Kazan to which Mlles. Moratief, Mme. Buscarlet's former pupils, went after her departure.

On the night of the 9th of December (O. S.) of the same year, Mme. Buscarlet had a dream which she described the following morning in a letter to Mme. Moratief, dated 10 December. She wrote, to quote her own words:

"You and I were on a country-road when a carriage passed in front of us and a voice from inside called to us. When we came up to the carriage, we saw Mlle. Olga Popoi lying across it, clothed in white, wearing a bonnet trimmed with yellow ribbons. She said to you:

" 'I called you to tell you that Mme. Nitchinof will leave the school on the 17th.'

"The carriage then drove on."

The Unknown Guest

A week later and three days before the letter reached Kazan, the event foreseen in the dream was fulfilled in a tragic fashion. Mme. Nitchinof died on the 16th of an infectious disease; and on the 17th her body was carried out of the school for fear of infection.

It is well to add that both Mme. Buscarlet's letter and the replies which came from Russia were communicated to Professor Flournoy and bear the postmark dates.

Such premonitory dreams are frequent; but it does not often happen that circumstances and especially the existence of a document dated previous to their fulfilment give them such incontestable authenticity.

We may remark in passing the odd character of this premonition, which however is fully in accordance with the habits of our unknown guest. The date is fixed precisely; but only a veiled and mysterious allusion (the woman lying across the carriage and cloaked in white) is made to the essential part of the prediction, the illness and death.

Was there a coincidence, a vision of the future pure and simple, or a vision of the future suggested by telepathic influence? The theory of coincidence can be defended, if need be, here as everywhere else, but would be very extraordinary in this case. As for telepathic influence, we should have to suppose that, on the 9th of December, a week before her death, Mme. Nitchinof had in her subconsciousness a presentiment of her end and that she transmitted this presentiment across some thousands of miles, from Kazan to Geneva, to a person with whom she had never been intimate. It is very complex, but possible, for telepathy often has these disconcerting ways. If this were so, the case which would be one of latent illness or even of self-suggestion; and the preexistence of the future, without being entirely disproved, would be less clearly established.

5

Let us pass to other examples. I quote from an excellent article on the importance of precognitions, by Messrs. Pickering and Sadgrove, which appeared in the *Annales des sciences psychiques* for 1 February 1908, the summary of an experiment by Mrs. A. W. Verrall told in full detail in Vol. XX of the *Proceedings*. Mrs. Verrall is a celebrated "automatist"; and her "cross-correspondences" occupy a whole volume of the *Proceedings*. Her good faith, her sincerity, her fairness and her scientific precision are above suspicion; and she is one of the most active and respected members of the Society for Psychical Research.

On the 11th of May, 1901, at 11.10 P.M., Mrs. Varrall wrote as follows:

"Do not hurry   date this   hoc est quod volui—tandem. δικαιοσύνη καὶ χαρὰ συμφωνεῖ συνετοῖσιν. A. W. V. καὶ ἄλλῳ τινὶ ἴσως. calx pedibus inhaerens difficultatem superavit. magnopere adiuvas persectando semper. Nomen inscribere iam possum—sic, en tibi!"[1]

After the writing comes a humorous drawing representing a bird walking.

That same night, as there were said to be "uncanny happenings" in some rooms near the London Law Courts, the watchers arranged to sit through the night in the empty rooms. Precautions were taken to prevent intrusion and powdered chalk was spread on the floor of the two smaller rooms, "to

---

[1] Xenoglossy is well known not to be unusual in automatic writing; sometimes even the "automatist" speaks or writes languages of which he is completely ignorant. The Latin and Greek passages are translated as follows:

"This is what I have wanted, at last. Justice and joy speak a word to the wise. A. W. V. and perhaps some one else. Chalk sticking to the feet has got over the difficulty. You help greatly by always persevering. Now I can write a name—thus, here it is!"

trace anybody or anything that might come or go." Mrs. Verrall knew nothing of the matter. The phenomena began at 12.43 A.M. and ended at 2.9 A.M. The watchers noticed marks on the powdered chalk. On examination it was seen that the marks were "clearly defined bird's footprints in the middle of the floor, three in the left-hand room and five in the right-hand room." The marks were identical and exactly 2¾ inches in width; they might be compared to the footprints of a bird about the size of a turkey. The footprints were observed at 2.30 A. M.; the unexplained phenomena had begun at 12.43 that same morning. The words about "chalk sticking to the feet" are a singularly appropriate comment on the events; but the remarkable point is that Mrs. Verrall wrote what we have said *one hour and thirty-three minutes before the events took place.*

The persons who watched in the two

rooms were questioned by Mr. J. G. Piddington, a member of the council of the S. P. R., and declared that they had not any expectation of what they discovered.

I need hardly add that Mrs. Verrall had never heard anything about the happenings in the haunted house and that the watchers were completely ignorant of Mrs. Verrall's existence.

Here then is a very curious prediction of an event, insignificant in itself, which is to happen, in a house unknown to the one who foretells it, to people whom she does not know either. The spiritualists, who score in this case, not without some reason, will have it that a spirit, in order to prove its existence and its intelligence, organized this little scene in which the future, the present and the past are all mixed up together. Are they right? Or is Mrs. Verrall's subconsciousness roaming like this, at random, in the future? It is certain that the problem has seldom appeared under a more baffling aspect.

6

We will now take another premonitory dream, strictly controlled by the committee of the S. P. R.[1] Early in September, 1893, Annette, wife of Walter Jones, tobacconist, of Old Gravel Lane, East London, had her little boy ill. One night she dreamt that she saw a cart drive up and stop near where she was. It contained three coffins, "two white and one blue. One white coffin was bigger than the other; and the blue was the biggest of the three." The driver took out the bigger white coffin and left it at the mother's feet, driving off with the others. Mrs. Jones told her dream to her husband and to a neighbour, laying particular stress on the curious circumstance that one of the coffins was blue.

[1] *Proceedings,* vol. xi., p. 493.

The Unknown Guest

On the 10th of September, a friend of Mr. and Mrs. Jones was confined of a boy, who died on the 29th of the same month. Their own little boy died on the following Monday, the 2nd of October, being then sixteen months old. It was decided to bury the two children on the same day. On the morning of the day chosen, the parish priest informed Mr. and Mrs. Jones that another child had died in the neighbourhood and that its body would be brought into church along with the two others. Mrs. Jones remarked to her husband:

"If the coffin is blue, then my dream will come true. For the two other coffins were white."

The third coffin was brought; it was blue. It remains to be observed that the dimensions of the coffins corresponded exactly with the dream premonitions, the smallest being that of the child who died first, the next that of the little Jones boy, who was sixteen months old, and the largest, the blue one, that of a boy six years of age.

Let us take, more or less at random, another case from the inexhaustible *Proceedings*.[1] The report is written by Mr. Alfred Cooper and attested by the Duchess of Hamilton, the Duke of Manchester and another gentleman to whom the duchess related the incident before the fulfilment of the prophetic vision:

"A fortnight before the death of the late Earl of L———," says Mr. Cooper, "in 1882, I called upon the Duke of Hamilton, in Hill Street, to see him professionally. After I had finished seeing him, we went into the drawing-room, where the duchess was, and the duke said to me:

" 'Oh, Cooper, how is the earl?'

"The duchess said, 'What earl?' and, on

my answering, 'Lord L———,' she replied:

" 'That is very odd. I have had a most extraordinary vision. I went to bed, but, after being in bed a short time, I was not exactly asleep, but thought I saw a scene as if from a play before me. The actors in it were Lord L———, in a chair, as if in a fit, with a man standing over him with a red beard. He was by the side of a bath, over which bath a red lamp was distinctly shown.'

"I then said:

" 'I am attending Lord L——— at present; there is very little the matter with him; he is not going to die; he will be all right very soon.'

"Well, he got better for a week and was nearly well, but, at the end of six or seven days after this, I was called to see him suddenly. He had inflammation of both lungs.

"I called in Sir William Jenner, but in

six days he was a dead man. There were two male nurses attending on him; one had been taken ill. But, when I saw the other, the dream of the duchess was exactly represented. He was standing near a bath over the earl and, strange to say, his beard was red. There was the bath with the red lamp over it; and this brought the story to my mind.

"The vision seen by the duchess was told two weeks before the death of Lord L⸺. It is a most remarkable thing."

7

But it is impossible to find space for the many instances related. As I have said, there are hundreds of them, making their tracks in every direction across the plains of the future. Those which I have quoted give a sufficient idea of the predominating tone and the general aspect of this sort of story. It is nevertheless right to add that many of them are not at all tragic and that premonition opens its mysterious and capricious vistas of the future in connection with the most diverse and insignificant events. It cares but little for the human value of the occurrence and puts the vision of a number in a lottery on the same plane as the most dramatic death. The roads by which it reaches us are also unexpected and varied. Often, as in the examples quoted, it comes to us in a dream. Sometimes, it is an auditory or visual hallucination which seizes upon us while awake; sometimes, an indefinable but clear and irresistible presentiment, a shapeless but powerful obsession, an absurd but imperative certainty which rises from the depths of our inner darkness, where perhaps lies hidden the final answer to every riddle.

One might illustrate each of these manifestations with numerous examples. I will mention only a few, selected not among the most striking or the most attractive, but among those which have been most strictly tested and investigated.[1] A young peasant from the neighbourhood of Ghent, two months before the drawing for the conscription, announces to all and sundry that he will draw number 90 from the urn. On entering the presence of the district-commissioner in charge, he asks if number 90 is still in. The answer is yes.

"Well, then, I shall have it!"

And, to the general amazement, he does draw number 90.

Questioned as to the manner in which he acquired this strange certainty, he declares that, two months ago, just after he had gone to bed, he saw a huge, indescribable form appear in a corner of his room, with the number 90 standing out plainly in the middle, in figures the size of a man's hand. He sat up in bed and shut and opened his

[1] *Proceedings,* vol. xi., p. 545.

eyes to persuade himself that he was not dreaming. The apparition remained in the same place, distinctly and undeniably.

Professor Georges Hulin, of the university of Ghent, and M. Jules van Dooren, the district-commissioner, who report the incident, mention three other similar and equally striking cases witnessed by M. van Dooren during his term of office. I am the less inclined to doubt their declaration inasmuch as I am personally acquainted with them and know that their statements, as regards the objective reality of the facts, are so to speak equivalent to a legal deposition. M. Bozzano mentions some previsions which are quite as remarkable in connection with the gaming-tables at Monte Carlo.

I repeat, I am aware that, in the case of these occurrences and those which resemble them, it is possible once again to invoke the theory of coincidence. It will be contended that there are probably a thousand predictions of this kind which are never talked about, because they were not fulfilled, whereas, if one of them is accomplished, which is bound by the law of probabilities to happen some day or other, the astonishment is general and free rein is given to the imagination. This is true; nevertheless, it is well to enquire whether these predictions are as frequent as is loosely stated. In the matter of those which concern the conscription-drawings, for instance, I have had the opportunity of interrogating more than one constant witness of these little dramas of fate; and all admitted that, on the whole, they are much rarer than one would believe. Next, we must not forget that there can be no question here of scientific proofs. We are in the midst of a slippery and nebulous region, where we would not dare to risk a step if we were not allowing ourselves to be guided by our feelings rather

137

than by certainties which we are not forbidden to hope for, but which are not yet
in sight.

8

We will abridge our subject still further,
referring readers who wish to know the details to the originals, lest we should never
have done; or rather, instead of attempt-
ing an abridgment, which would still be
too long, so plentiful are the materials, we
will content ourselves with enumerating a
few instances, all taken from Bozzano's
Des Phénomènes prémonitoires. We read
there of a funeral procession seen on a high-
road several days before it actually passed
that way; or, again, of a young mechanic
who, in the beginning of November,
dreamt that he came home at half-past five
in the afternoon and saw his sister's little
girl run over by a tram-car while crossing
the street in front of the house. He told

his dream, in great distress; and, on the 13th of the same month, in spite of all the precautions that had been taken, the child was run over by the tram-car and killed at the hour named. We find the ghost, the phantom animal or the mysterious noise which, in certain families, is the traditional herald of a death or of an imminent catastrophe. We find the celebrated vision which the painter Segantini had thirteen days before his decease, every detail of which remained in his mind and was represented in his last picture, *Death*. We find the Messina disaster clearly foreseen, twice over, by a little girl who perished under the ruins of the ill-fated city; and we read of a dream which, three months before the French invasion of Russia, foretold to Countess Toutschkoff that her husband would fall at Borodino, a village so little known at the time that those interested in the dream looked in vain for its name on the maps.

Until now we have spoken only of the spontaneous manifestations of the future. It would seem as though coming events, gathered in front of our lives, bear with crushing weight upon the uncertain and deceptive dike of the present, which is no longer able to contain them. They ooze through, they seek a crevice by which to reach us. But, side by side with these passive, independent and intractable premonitions, which are but so many vagrant and furtive emanations of the unknown, are others which do yield to entreaty, allow themselves to be directed into channels, are more or less obedient to our orders and will sometimes reply to the questions which we put to them. They come from the same inaccessible reservoir, are no less mysterious, but yet appear a little more human than the others; and, without drugging ourselves with puerile or dangerous illusions, we may be permitted to hope that, if we follow

them and study them attentively, they will
one day open to us the hidden paths that
join that which is no more to that which is
not yet.

It is true that here, where we must needs
mix with the somewhat lawless world of
professional mystery-mongers, we have to
increase our caution and walk with measured steps on very suspicious ground. But
even in this region of pitfalls we glean a certain number of facts that cannot reason-
ably be contested. It will be enough to
recall, for instance, the symbolic premonitions of the famous "seeress of Prevorst,"
Frau Hauffe, whose prophetic spirit was
awakened by soap-bubbles, crystals and mirrors;[1] the clairvoyant who, eighteen years
before the event, foretold the death of a
girl by the hand of her rival in 1907, in a
written prophecy which was presented to
the court by the mother of the murdered

[1] A. J. C. Kerner: *Die Scherin von Prevorst.*

girl;[1] the gypsy who, also in writing, foretold all the events in Miss Isabel Arundel's
life, including the name of her husband,
Burton, the famous explorer;[2] the sealed
letter addressed to M. Morin, vice-president of the Société du Mesmerisme, describing the most unexpected circumstances
of a death that occurred a month later;[3]
the famous "Marmontel prediction," obtained by Mrs. Verrall's cross-correspondences, which gives a vision, two months and
a half before their accomplishment, of the
most insignificant actions of a traveller in
an hotel bedroom;[4] and many others.

9

I will not review the various and very

[1] *Light,* 1907, p. 219. The crime was committed in
Paris and made a great stir at the time.

[2] LADY BURTON: *The Life of Captain Sir Richd. F.
Burton, K.C.M.G.,* vol. i., p. 253.

[3] *Journal of the Society for Psychical Research,* vol.
ix., p. 15.

[4] *Proceedings,* vol. xx., p. 331.

often grotesque methods of interrogating
the future that are most frequently practised to-day: cards, palmistry, crystal-
gazing, fortune-telling by means of coffee-
grounds, tea-leaves, magnetic needles and
white of egg, graphology, astrology and
the rest. These methods, as I have already
said, are worth exactly what the medium
who employs them is worth. They have
no other object than to arouse the medium's
subconsciousness and to bring it into relation with that of the person questioning
him. As a matter of fact, all these purely
empirical processes are but so many, often
puerile forms of self-manifestation adopted
by the undeniable gift which is known as
intuition, clairvoyance or, in certain cases,
psychometry. I have spoken at sufficient
length of this last faculty not to linger over
it now. All that we have still to do is to
consider it for a moment in its relations
with the foretelling of the future.

The Unknown Guest

A large number of investigations, notably those conducted by M. Duchatel and Dr. Osty, show that, in psychometry, the notion of time, as Dr. Joseph Maxwell observes, is very loose, that is to say, the past, present and future nearly always overlap. Most of the clairvoyant or psychometric subjects, when they are honest, do not know, "do not feel," as M. Duchatel very ably remarks, "what the future is. They do not distinguish it from the other tenses; and consequently they succeed in being prophets, but unconscious prophets." In a word—and this is a very important indication from the point of view of the probable coexistence of the three tenses—it appears that they see that which is not yet with the same clearness and on the same plane as that which is no more, but are incapable of separating the two visions and picking out the future which alone interests us. For a still stronger rea-

son, it is impossible for them to state dates
with precision. Nevertheless, the fact remains that, when we take the trouble to
sift their evidence and have the patience to
await the realization of certain events
which are sometimes not due for a long
time to come, the future is fairly often perceived by some of these strange sooth-
sayers.

There are psychometers, however, and
notably Mme. M——, Dr. Osty's favourite medium, who never confuse the future
and the past. Mme. M—— places her visions in time according to the position
which they occupy in space. Thus she sees
the future in front of her, the past behind
her and the present beside her. But, notwithstanding these distinctly-graded visions,
she also is incapable of naming her dates
exactly; in fact, her mistakes in this respect
are so general that Dr. Osty looks upon it
as a pure chronological coincidence when a

prediction is realized at the moment foretold.

We should also observe that, in psychometry, only those events can be perceived which relate directly to the individual communicating with the percipient, for it is not so much the percipient that sees into us as we that read in our own subconsciousness, which is momentarily lighted by his presence. We must not therefore ask him for predictions of a general character, whether, for instance, there will be a war in the spring, an epidemic in the summer or an earthquake in the autumn. The moment the question concerns events, however important, with which we are not intimately connected, he is bound to answer, as do all the genuine mediums, that he sees nothing.

The area of his vision being thus limited, does he really discover the future in it? After three years of numerous, cautious and systematic experiments with some twenty mediums, Dr. Osty categorically declares that he does:

"All the incidents," he says, "which filled these three years of my life, whether wished for by me or not, or even absolutely contrary to the ordinary routine of my life, had always been foretold to me, not all by each of the clairvoyant subjects, but all by one or other of them. As I have been practising these tests continually, it seems to me that the experience of three years wholly devoted to this object should give some weight to my opinion on the subject of predictions."

This is incontestable; and the sincerity, scientific conscientiousness and high intellectual value of Dr. Osty's fine work inspire one with the most entire confidence. Unfortunately, he contents himself with quoting too summarily a few facts and does not, as he ought, give us *in extenso* the de-

tails of his experiments, controls and tests.
I am well aware that this would be a thankless and wearisome task, necessitating a
large volume which a mass of puerile incidents and inevitable repetitions would make
almost unreadable. Moreover, it could
scarcely help taking the form of an intimate and indiscreet autobiography; and it
is not easy to bring one's self to make this
sort of public confession. But it has to be
done. In a science which is only in its early
stages, it is not enough to show the object
attained and to state one's conviction; it is
necessary above all to describe every path
that has been taken and, by an incessant
and infinite accumulation of investigated
and attested facts, to enable every one to
draw his own conclusions. This has been
the cumbrous and laborious method of the
Proceedings for over thirty years; and it
is the only right one. Discussion is possible and fruitful only at that price. In all

these extraconscious matters, we have not yet reached the stage of definite deductions, we are still bringing up materials to the scene of operations.

Once more, I know that, in these cases, as I have seen for myself, the really convincing facts are necessarily very rare; indeed, nowhere else do we meet with the same difficulty. If the medium tells you, for instance, as Mme. M—— seems easily to do, how you will employ your day from the morning onwards, if she sees you in a certain house in a certain street meeting this or that person, it is impossible to say that, on the one hand, she is not already reading your as yet unconscious plans or intentions, or that, on the other hand, by doing what she has foreseen, you are not obeying a suggestion against which you could not fight except by violently doing the opposite to what it demands of you, which again would be a case of inverted suggestion. None

149

therefore would have any value save predictions of unlikely happenings, clearly defined and outside the sphere of the person interested. As Dr. Osty says:

"The ideal prognostication would obviously be that of an event so rare, so sudden and unexpected, implying such a change in one's mode of life that the theory of coincidence could not decently be put forward. But, as everybody is not, in the peaceful course of his existence, threatened by such an absolutely convincing event, the clairvoyant cannot always reveal to the person experimenting—and reveal it for a more or less approximate date—one of those incidents whose accomplishment would carry irresistible conviction."

In any case, the question of psychometric prognostications calls for further enquiry, although it is easy even at the present day to foresee the results.

10

Let us now return to our spontaneous premonitions, in which the future comes to seek us of its own accord and, so to speak, to challenge us at home. I know from personal experience that, when we embark upon these disconcerting matters, the first impression is scarcely favourable. We are very much inclined to laugh, to treat as wearisome tales, as hysterical hallucinations, as ingenious or interested fictions most of those incidents which give too violent a shock to the narrow and limited idea which we have of our human life. To smile, to reject everything beforehand and to pass by with averted head, as was done, remember, in the time of Galvani and in the early days of hypnotism, is much more easy and seems more respectable and prudent than to stop, admit and examine. Nevertheless we must not forget that it is to some who did not smile so lightly that we owe the best part of the marvels from whose heights we are preparing to smile in our turn. For the rest, I grant that, thus presented, hastily and summarily, without the details that throw light upon them and the proofs that support them, the incidents in question do not show to advantage and, inasmuch as they are isolated and sparingly chosen, lose all the weight and authority derived from the compact and imposing mass whence they are arbitrarily detached. As I said above, nearly a thousand cases have been collected, representing probably not the tenth part of those which a more active and general search might bring together. The number is evidently of importance and denotes the enormous pressure of the mystery; but, if there were only half a dozen genuine cases—and Dr. Maxwell's, Professor Flournoy's, Mrs. Verrall's, the Marmontel, Jones and Hamilton cases and some others are undoubtedly

152

genuine—they would be enough to show that, under the erroneous idea which we form of the past and the present, a new verity is living and moving, eager to come to light.

The efforts of that verity, I need hardly say, display a very different sort of force after we have actually and attentively read those hundreds of extraordinary stories which, without appearing to do so, strike to the very roots of history. We soon lose all inclination to doubt. We penetrate into another world and come to a stop all out of countenance. We no longer know where we stand; before and after overlap and mingle. We no longer distinguish the insidious and factitious but indispensable line which separates the years that have gone by from the years that are to come. We clutch at the hours and days of the past and present to reassure ourselves, to fasten on to some certainty, to convince ourselves that we are still in our right place in this life where that which is not yet seems as substantial, as real, as positive, as powerful as that which is no more. We discover with uneasiness that time, on which we based our whole existence, itself no longer exists. It is no longer the swiftest of our gods, known to us only by its flight across all things; it alters its position no more than space, of which it is doubtless but the incomprehensible reflex. It reigns in the centre of every event; and every event is fixed in its centre; and all that comes and all that goes passes from end to end of our little life without moving by a hair's breadth around its motionless pivot. It is entitled to but one of the thousand names which we have been wont to lavish upon its power, a power that seemed to us manifold and innumerable: yesterday, recently, formerly, erewhile, after, before, to-morrow, soon, never, later fall like childish masks, whereas to-day and always completely cover with their united shadows the idea which we form in the end of a duration which has no subdivisions, no breaks and no stages, which is pulseless, motionless and boundless.

II

Many are the theories which men have imagined in their attempts to explain the working of the strange phenomenon; and many others might be imagined.

As we have seen, self-suggestion and telepathy explain certain cases which concern events already in existence, but still latent and perceived before the knowledge of them can reach us by the normal process of the senses or the intelligence. But, even by extending these two theories to their uttermost point and positively abusing their accommodating elasticity, we do not succeed in illumining by their aid more than a

rather restricted portion of the vast undis-
covered land. We must therefore look for
something else.

The first theory which suggests itself and
which on the surface seems rather attractive
is that of spiritualism, which may be extended until it is scarcely distinguishable
from the theosophical theory and other religious suppositions. It assumes the survival of spirits, the existence of discarnate
or other superior and more mysterious entities which surround us, interest themselves
in our fate, guide our thoughts and our actions and, above all, know the future. It
is, as we recognized when speaking of
ghosts and hanted houses, a very acceptable
theory; and any one to whom it appears
can adopt it without doing violence to his
intelligence. But we must confess that it
seems less necessary and perhaps even less
clearly proved in this region than in that.
It starts by begging the question: without

the intervention of discarnate beings, the spiritualists say, it is impossible to explain the majority of the premonitory phenomena; therefore we must admit the existence of these discarnate beings. Let us grant it for the moment, for to beg the question, which is merely an indefensible trick of the superficial logic of our brain, does not necessarily condemn a theory and neither takes away from nor adds to the reality of things. Besides, as we shall insist later, the intervention or non-intervention of the spirits is not the point at issue; and the crux of the mystery does not lie there. What must interest us is far less the paths or intermediaries by which prophetic warnings reach us than the actual existence of the future in the present. It is true—to do complete justice to neospiritualism—that its position offers certain advantages from the point of view of the almost inconceivable problem of the preexistence of the future. It can evade or divert some of the consequences of that problem. The spirits, it declares, do not necessarily see the future as a whole, as a total past or present, motionless and immovable, but they know infinitely better than we do the numberless causes that determine any agent, so that, finding themselves at the luminous source of those causes, they have no difficulty in foreseeing their effects. They are, with respect to the incidents still in process of formation, in the position of an astronomer who foretells, within a second, all the phases of an eclipse in which a savage sees nothing but an unprecedented catastrophe which he attributes to the anger of his idols of straw or clay. It is indeed possible that this acquaintance with a greater number of causes explains certain predictions; but there are plenty of others which presume a knowledge of so many causes, causes so remote and so profound, that this knowledge

is hardly to be distinguished from a knowledge of the future pure and simple. In any
case, beyond certain limits, the preexistence
of causes seems no clearer than that of effects. Nevertheless, it must be admitted
that the spiritualists gain a slight advantage
here.

They believe that they gain another
when they say or might say that it is still
possible that the spirits stimulate us
to realize the events which they foretell
without themselves clearly perceiving them
in the future. After announcing, for instance, that on a certain day we shall go to
a certain place and do a certain thing, they
urge us irresistibly to proceed to the spot
named and there to perform the act
prophesied. But this theory, like those of
self-suggestion and telepathy, would explain only a few phenomena and would
leave in obscurity all those cases, infinitely
more numerous because they make up al-

most the whole of our future, in which either chance intervenes or some event in no way dependent upon our will or the spirit's, unless indeed we suppose that the latter possesses an omniscience and an omnipotence which take us back to the original mysteries of the problem.

Besides, in the gloomy regions of precognition, it is almost always a matter of anticipating a misfortune and very rarely, if ever, of meeting with a pleasure or a joy. We should therefore have to admit that the spirits which drag me to the fatal place and compel me to do the act that will have tragic consequences are deliberately hostile to me and find diversion only in the spectacle of my suffering. What could those spirits be, from what evil world would they arise and how should we explain why our brothers and friends of yesterday, after passing through the august and peace-bestowing gates of death, suddenly become transformed into crafty and malevolent demons? Can the great spiritual kingdom, in which all passions born of the flesh should be stilled, be but a dismal abode of hatred, spite and envy? It will perhaps be said that they lead us into misfortune in order to purify us; but this brings us to religious theories which it is not our intention to examine.

12

The only attempt at an explanation that can hold its own with spiritualism has recourse once again to the mysterious powers of our subconsciousness. We must needs recognize that, if the future exists to-day, already such as it will be when it becomes for us the present and the past, the intervention of discarnate minds or of any other spiritual entity adrift from another sphere is of little avail. We can picture an infinite spirit indifferently contemplating the past and future in their co-existence; we can imagine a whole hierarchy of intermediate intelligences taking a more or less extensive part in the contemplation and transmitting it to our subconsciousness. But all this is practically nothing more than inconsistent speculation and ingenious dreaming in the dark; in any case, it is adventitious, secondary and provisional. Let us keep to the facts as we see them: an unknown faculty, buried deep in our being and generally inactive, perceives, on rare occasions, events that have not yet taken place. We possess but one certainty on this subject, namely, that the phenomenon actually occurs within ourselves; it is therefore within ourselves that we must first study it, without burdening ourselves with suppositions which remove it from its centre and simply shift the mystery. The incomprehensible mystery is the preexistence of the future; once we admit this—and it seems very difficult to deny—there is no reason to attribute to imaginary intermediaries rather than to ourselves the faculty of descrying certain fragments of that future. We see, in regard to most of the mediumistic manifestations, that we possess within ourselves all the unusual forces with which the spiritualists endow discarnate spirits; and why should it be otherwise as concerns the powers of divination? The explanation taken from the subconsciousness is the most direct, the simplest, the nearest, whereas the other is endlessly circuitous, complicated and distant. Until the spirits testify to their existence in an unanswerable fashion, there is no advantage in seeking in the grave for the solution of a riddle that appears indeed to lie at the roots of our own life.

13

It is true that this explanation does not explain much; but the others are just as ineffectual and are open to the same objections. These objections are many and various; and it is easier to raise them than to reply to them. For instance, we can ask ourselves why the subconsciousness or the spirits, seeing that they read the future and are able to announce an impending calamity, hardly ever give us the one useful and definite indication that would allow us to avoid it. What can be the childish or mysterious reason of this strange reticence? In many cases it is almost criminal; for instance, in a case related by Professor Hyslop[1] we see the foreboding of the greatest misfortune that can befall a mother germinating, growing, sending out shoots, developing, like some gluttonous and deadly plant, to stop short on the verge of the last warning, the one detail, insignificant in itself but indispensable, which would have saved the child. It is the case

[1]*Proceedings,* vol. xiv., p. 266.

of a woman who begins by experiencing a vague but powerful impression that a grievous "burden" was going to fall upon her family. Next month, this premonitory feeling repeats itself very frequently, becomes more intense and ends by concentrating itself upon the poor woman's little daughter. Each time that she is planning something for the child's future, she hears a voice saying:

"She'll never need it."

A week before the catastrophe, a violent smell of fire fills the house. From that time the mother begins to be careful about matches, seeing that they are in safe places and out of reach. She looks all over the house for them and feels a strong impulse to burn all matches of the kind easily lighted. About an hour before the fatal disaster, she reaches for a box to destroy it; but she says to herself that her eldest boy is gone out, thinks that she may need the

matches to light the gas-stove and decides
to destroy them as soon as he comes back.
She takes the child up to its crib for its
morning sleep and, as she is putting it into
the cradle, she hears the usual mysterious
voice whisper in her ear:

"Turn the mattress."

But, being in a great hurry, she simply
says that she will turn the mattress after
the child has taken its nap. She then goes
downstairs to work. After a while, she
hears the child cry and, hurrying up to the
room, finds the crib and its bedding on fire
and the child so badly burnt that it dies
in three hours.

14

Before going further and theorizing
about this case, let us once more state the
matter precisely. I know that the reader
may straightway and quite legitimately
deny the value of anecdotes of this kind.

The Unknown Guest

He will say that we have to do with a neurotic who has drawn upon her imagination for all the elements that give a dramatic setting to the story and surround with a halo of mystery a sad but commonplace domestic accident. This is quite possible; and it is perfectly allowable to dismiss the case. But it is none the less true that, by thus deliberately rejecting everything that does not bear the stamp of mathematical or judicial certainty, we risk losing as we go along most of the opportunities or clues which the great riddle of this world offers us in its moments of inattention or graciousness. At the beginning of an enquiry we must know how to content ourselves with little. For the incident in question to be convincing, previous evidence in writing, more or less official statements, would be required, whereas we have only the declarations of the husband, a neighbour and a sister. This is insufficient, I agree; but we must at the same time confess that the circumstances are hardly favourable to obtaining the proofs which we demand. Those who receive warnings of this kind either believe in them or do not believe in them. If they believe in them, it is quite natural that they should not think first of all of the scientific interest of their trouble, or of putting down in writing and thus authenticating its premonitory symptoms and gradual evolution. If they do not believe in them, it is no less natural that they should not proceed to speak or take notice of inanities of which they do not recognize the value until after they have lost the opportunity of supplying convincing proofs of them. Also, do not forget that the little story in question is selected from among a hundred others, which in their turn are equally indecisive, but which, repeating the same facts and the same tendencies with a strange persistency, and by weakening the most inveterate distrust.[1]

15

Having said this much, in order to conciliate or part company with those who have no intention of leaving the *terra firma* of science, let us return to the case before us, which is all the more disquieting inasmuch as we may consider it a sort of prototype of the tragic and almost diabolical reticence which we find in most premonitions. It is probable that under the mattress there was a stray match which the child discovered and struck; this is the only possible explanation of the catastrophe, for there was no fire burning on that floor of the house. If the mother had turned the mattress, she would have seen the match;

[1]See, in particular, Bozzano's cases xlix. and lxvii. These two, especially case xlix., which tells of a personal experience of the late W. T. Stead, are supported by more substantial proofs. I have quoted Professor Hyslop's case, because the reticence is more striking.

and, on the other hand, she would certainly have turned the mattress if she had been told that there was a match underneath it. Why did the voice that urged her to perform the necessary action not add the one word that was capable of ensuring that action? The problem moreover is equally perturbing and perhaps equally insoluble whether it concerns our own subconscious faculties, or spirits, or strange intelligences. Those who give these warnings must know that they will be useless, because they manifestly foresee the event as a whole; but they must also know that one last word, which they do not pronounce, would be enough to prevent the misfortune that is already consummated in their prevision. They know it so well that they bring this word to the very edge of the abyss, hold it suspended there, almost let it fall and recapture it suddenly at the moment when its weight would have caused happiness and life to rise once more to the surface of the mighty gulf. What then is this mystery? Is it incapacity or hostility? If they are incapable, what is the unexpected and sovran force that interposes between them and us? And, if they are hostile, on what, on whom are they revenging themselves? What can be the secret of those inhuman games, of those uncanny and cruel diversions on the most slippery and dangerous peaks of fate? Why warn, if they know that the warning will be in vain? Of whom are they making sport? Is there really an inflexible fatality by virtue of which that which has to be accomplished is accomplished from all eternity? But then why not respect silence, since all speech is useless? Or do they, in spite of all, perceive a gleam, a crevice in the inexorable wall? What hope do they find in it? Have they not seen more clearly than ourselves that no deliverance can come through that crevice? One could understand this fluttering and wavering, all these efforts of theirs, if they did not know; but here it is proved that they know everything, since they foretell exactly that which they might prevent. If we press them with questions, they answer that there is nothing to be done, that no human power could avert or thwart the issue. Are they mad, bored, irritable, or accessory to a hideous pleasantry? Does our fate depend on the happy solution of some petty enigma or childish conundrum, even as our salvation, in most of the so-called revealed religions, is settled by a blind and stupid cast of the die? Is all the liberty that we are granted reduced to the reading of a more or less ingenious riddle? Can the great soul of the universe be the soul of a great baby?

16

But, rather than pursue this subject, let

us be just and admit that there is perhaps no way out of the maze and that our reproaches are as incomprehensible as the conduct of the spirits. Indeed, what would you have them do in the circle in which our logic imprisons them? Either they foretell us a calamity which their predictions cannot avert, in which case there is no use in foretelling it, or, if they announce it to us and at the same time give us the means to prevent it, they do not really see the future and are foretelling nothing, since the calamity is not to take place, with the result that their action seems equally absurd in both cases.

It is obvious: to whichever side we turn, we find nothing but the incomprehensible. On the one hand, the preestablished, unshakable, unalterable future which we have called destiny, fatality or what you will, which suppresses man's entire independence and liberty of action and which is the most

inconceivable and the dreariest of mysteries; on the other, intelligences apparently
superior to our own, since they know what
we do not, which, while aware that their
intervention is always useless and very
often cruel, nevertheless come harassing us
with their sinister and ridiculous predictions. Must we resign ourselves once more
to living with our eyes shut and our reason
drowned in the boundless ocean of darkness; and is there no outlet?

17

For the moment we will not linger in
the dark regions of fatality, which is the
supreme mystery, the desolation of every
effort and every thought of man. What
is clearest amid this incomprehensibility is
that the spiritualistic theory, at first sight
the most seductive, declares itself, on examination, the most difficult to justify. We
will also once more put aside the theosophi-

cal theory or any other which assumes a
divine intention and which might, to a certain extent, explain the hesitations and
anguish of the prophetic warnings, at the
cost, however, of other puzzles, a thousand
times as hard to solve, which nothing au-
thorizes us to substitute for the actual puzzle, formless and infinite, presented to our
uninitiated vision.

When all is said, it is perhaps only in the
theory which attributes those premonitions
to our subconsciousness that we are able to
find, if not a justification, at least a sort of
explanation of that formidable reticence.
They accord fairly well with the strange,
inconsistent, whimsical and disconcerting
character of the unknown entity within
us that seems to live on nothing but
nondescript fare borrowed from worlds to
which our intelligence as yet has no access.
It lives under our reason, in a sort of invisible and perhaps eternal palace, like a

casual guest, dropped from another planet, whose interests, ideas, habits, passions have naught in common with ours. If it seems to have notions on the hereafter that are infinitely wider and more precise than those which we possess, it has only very vague notions on the practical needs of our existence. It ignores us for years, absorbed no doubt with the numberless relations which it maintains with all the mysteries of the universe; and, when suddenly it remembers us, thinking apparently to please us, it makes an enormous, miraculous, but at the same time clumsy and superfluous movement, which upsets all that we believed we knew, without teaching us anything. Is it making fun of us, is it jesting, is it amusing itself, is it facetious, teasing, arch, or simply sleepy, bewildered, inconsistent, absent-minded? In any case, it is rather remarkable that it evidently dislikes to make itself useful. It readily performs the most glamorous feats of sleight-of-hand, provided that we can derive no profit from them. It lifts up tables, moves the heaviest articles, produces flowers and hair, sets strings vibrating, gives life to inanimate objects and passes through solid matter, conjures up ghosts, subjugates time and space, creates light; but all, it seems, on one condition, that its performances should be without rhyme or reason and keep to the province of supernaturally vain and puerile recreations. The case of the divining-rod is almost the only one in which it lends us any regular assistance, this being a sort of game, of no great importance, in which it appears to take pleasure. Sometimes, to say all that can be said, it consents to cure certain ailments, cleanses an ulcer, closes a wound, heals a lung, strengthens or makes supple an arm or leg, or even sets bones, but always as it were by accident, without reason, method or object, in a deceitful,

177

illogical and preposterous fashion. One would set it down as a spoilt child that has been allowed to lay hands on the most tremendous secrets of heaven and earth; it has no suspicion of their power, jumbles them all up together and turns them into paltry, inoffensive toys. It knows everything, perhaps, but is ignorant of the uses of its knowledge. It has its arms laden with treasures which it scatters in the wrong manner and at the wrong time, giving bread to the thirsty and water to the hungry, overloading those who refuse and stripping the suppliant bare, pursuing those who flee from it and fleeing from those who pursue it. Lastly, even at its best moments, it behaves as though the fate of the being in whose depths it dwells interested it hardly at all, as though it had but an insignificant share in his misfortunes, feeling assured, one might almost think, of an independent and endless existence.

It is not surprising, therefore, when we know its habits, that its communications on the subject of the future should be as fantastic as the other manifestations of its knowledge or its power. Let us add, to be quite fair, that, in those warnings which we would wish to see efficacious, it stumbles against the same difficulties as the spirits or other alien intelligences uselessly foretelling the event which they cannot prevent, or annihilating the event by the very fact of foretelling it.

18

And now, to end the question, is our unknown guest alone responsible? Does it explain itself badly or do we not understand it? When we look into the matter closely, there is, under those anomalous and confused manifestations, in spite of efforts which we feel to be enormous and persevering, a sort of incapacity for self-expression and action which is bound to attract our attention. Is our conscious and individual life separated by impenetrable worlds from our subconscious and probably universal life? Does our unknown guest speak an unknown language and do the words which it speaks and which we think that we understand disclose its thought? Is every direct road pitilessly barred and is there nothing left to it but narrow, closed paths in which the best of what it had to reveal to us is lost? Is this the reason why it seeks those odd, childish, roundabout ways of automatic writing, cross-correspondence, symbolic premonition and all the rest? Yet, in the typical case which we have quoted, it seems to speak quite easily and plainly when it says to the mother:

"Turn the mattress."

If it can utter this sentence, why should it find it difficult or impossible to add:

"You will find the matches there that will set fire to the curtains."

What forbids it to do so and closes its mouth at the decisive moment? We relapse into the everlasting question: if it cannot complete the second sentence because it would be destroying in the womb the very event which it is foretelling, why does it utter the first?

19

But it is well in spite of everything to seek an explanation of the inexplicable; it is by attacking it on every side, at all hazards, that we cherish the hope of overcoming it; and we may therefore say to ourselves that our subconsciousness, when it warns us of a calamity that is about to fall upon us, knowing all the future as it does, necessarily knows that the calamity is already accomplished. As our conscious and unconscious lives blend in it, it distresses it-

self and flutters around our overconfident
ignorance. It tries to inform us, through
nervousness, through pity, so as to mitigate
the lightning cruelty of the blow. It speaks
all the words that can prepare us for its
coming, define it and identify it; but it is
unable to say those which would prevent
it from coming, seeing that it has come,
that it is already present and perhaps past,
manifest, ineffaceable, on another plane
than that on which we live, the only plane
which we are capable of perceiving. It
finds itself, in a word, in the position of
the man who, in the midst of peaceful,
happy and unsuspecting folk, alone knows
some bad news. He is neither able nor
willing to announce it nor yet to hide it
completely. He hesitates, delays, makes
more or less transparent allusions, but does
not either say the last word that would, so
to speak, let loose the catastrophe in the
hearts of the people around him, for to

those who do not know of it the catastrophe
is still as though it were not there. Our
subconsciousness, in that case, would act
towards the future as we act towards the
past, the two conditions being identical, so
much so that it often confuses them, as
we can see more particularly in the celebrated Marmontel case, where it evidently
blunders and reports as accomplished an
incident that will not take place until several
months later. It is of course impossible
for us, at the stage which we have reached,
to understand this confusion or this coexistence of the past, the present and the future;
but that is no reason for denying it; on the
contrary, what man understands least is
probably that which most nearly approaches
the truth.

20

Lastly, to complicate the question, it may
be very justly objected that, though pre-

monitions in general are useless and appear systematically to withhold the only indispensable and decisive words, there are, nevertheless, some that often seem to save those who obey them. These, it is true, are rarer than the first, but still they include a certain number that are well-authenticated. It remains to be seen how far they imply a knowledge of the future.

Here, for instance, is a traveller who, arriving at night in a small unknown town and walking along the ill-lighted dock in the direction of an hotel of which he roughly knows the position, at a given moment feels an irresistible impulse to turn and go the other way. He instantly obeys, though his reason protests and "berates him for a fool" in taking a roundabout way to his destination. The next day he discovers that, if he had gone a few feet farther, he would certainly have slipped into the river; and, as he was but a feeble swimmer, he would just as certainly, being alone and un-aided in the extreme darkness, have been drowned.[1]

But is this a prevision of an event? No, for no event is to take place. There is simply an abnormal perception of the prox-imity of some unknown water and conse-quently of an imminent danger, an unex-plained but fairly frequent subliminal sensi-tiveness. In a word, the problem of the future is not raised in this case, nor in any of the numerous cases that resemble it.

Here is another which evidently belongs to the same class, though at first sight it seems to postulate the preexistence of a fatal event and a vision of the future cor-responding exactly with a vision of the past. A traveller in South America is descending a river in a canoe; the party are just about to run close to a promontory when a sort of mysterious voice, which he has already

[1] *Proceedings,* vol. xi., p. 422.

heard at different momentous times of his life, imperiously orders him immediately to cross the river and gain the other shore as quickly as possible. This appears so absurd that he is obliged to threaten the Indians with death to force them to take this course. They have scarcely crossed more than half the river when the promontory falls at the very place where they meant to round it.[1]

The perception of imminent danger is here, I admit, even more abnormal than in the previous example, but it comes under the same heading. It is a phenomenon of subliminal hypersensitiveness observed more than once, a sort of premonition induced by subconscious perceptions, which has been christened by the barbarous name of "cryptæsthesia." But the interval between the moment when the peril is signalled and that at which it is consummated

[1] FLOURNOY: *Esprits et médiums,* p. 316.

is too short for those questions which relate to a knowledge or a preexistence of the future to arise in this instance.

The case is almost the same with the adventure of an American dentist, very carefully investigated by Dr. Hodgson. The dentist was bending over a bench on which was a little copper in which he was vulcanizing some rubber, when he heard a voice calling, in a quick and imperative manner, these words:

"Run to the window, quick! Run to the window, quick!"

He at once ran to the window and looked out to the street below, when suddenly he heard a tremendous report and, looking round, saw that the copper had exploded, destroying a great part of the workroom.[1]

Here again, a subconscious cautiousness was probably aroused by certain indications imperceptible to our ordinary senses. It is

[1] *Proceedings*, vol. xi., p. 424.

even possible that there exists between things and ourselves a sort of sympathy or subliminal communion which makes us experience the trials and emotions of matter that has reached the limits of its existence, unless, as is more likely, there is merely a simple coincidence between the chance idea of a possible explosion and its realization.

A last and rather more complicated case is that of Jean Dupré, the sculptor, who was driving alone with his wife along a mountain road, skirting a perpendicular cliff. Suddenly they both heard a voice that seemed to come from the mountain crying:

"Stop!"

They turned round, saw nobody and continued their road. But the cries were repeated again and again, without anything to reveal the presence of a human being amid the solitude. At last the sculptor alighted and saw that the left wheel of the carriage, which was grazing the edge of the precipice, had lost its linch-pin and was on the point of leaving the axle-tree, which would almost inevitably have hurled the carriage into the abyss.

Need we, even here, relinquish the theory of subconscious perceptions? Do we know and can the author of the anecdote, whose good faith is not in question, tell us that certain unperceived circumstances, such as the grating of the wheel or the swaying of the carriage, did not give him the first alarm? After all, we know how easily stories of this kind involuntarily take a dramatic turn even at the actual moment and especially afterwards.

21

These examples—and there are many more of a similar kind—are enough, I think, to illustrate this class of premonitions. The problem in these cases is simpler than when it relates to fruitless warnings;

at least it is simpler so long as we do not bring into discussion the question of spirits, of unknown intelligences, or of an actual knowledge of the future; otherwise the same difficulty reappears and the warning, which this time seems efficacious, is in reality just as vain. In fact, the mysterious entity which knows that the traveller will go to the water's edge, that the wheel will be on the point of leaving the axle, that the copper will explode, or that the promontory will fall at a precise moment, must at the same time know that the traveller will not take the last fatal step, that the carriage will not be overturned, that the copper will not hurt anybody and that the canoe will pull away from the promontory. It is inadmissible that, seeing one thing, it will not see the other, since everything happens at the same point, in the course of the same second. Can we say that, if it had not given warning, the little saving movement

would not have been executed? How can
we imagine a future which, at one and the
same time, has parts that are steadfast and
others that are not? If it is foreseen that
the promontory will fall and that the
traveller will escape, thanks to the supernatural warning, it is necessarily foreseen
that the warning will be given; and, if so,
what is the point of this futile comedy?
I see no reasonable explanation of it in the
spiritist or spiritualistic theory, which postu-
lates a complete knowledge of the future,
at least at a settled point and moment. On
the other hand, if we adhere to the theory
of a subliminal consciousness, we find there
an explanation which is quite worthy of
acceptance. This subliminal consciousness,
though, in the majority of cases, it has no
clear and comprehensive vision of the immediate future, can nevertheless possess
an intuition of imminent danger, thanks to
indications that escape our ordinary percep-

tion. It can also have a partial, intermittent and so to speak flickering vision of the future event and, if doubtful, can risk giving an incoherent warning, which, for that matter, will change nothing in that which already is.

22

In conclusion, let us state once more that fruitful premonitions necessarily annihilate events in the bud and consequently work their own destruction, so that any control becomes impossible. They would have an existence only if they prophesied a general event which the subject would not escape but for the warning. If they had said to any one intending to go to Messina two or three months before the catastrophe, "Don't go, for the town will be destroyed before the month is out," we should have an excellent example. But it is a remarkable thing that genuine premonitions of this kind are very rare and nearly always rather indefinite in regard to events of a general order. In M. Bozzano's excellent collection, which is a sort of compendium of premonitory phenomena, the only pretty clear cases are nos. clv. and clviii., both of which are taken from the *Journal of the S.P.R.* In the first,[1] a mother sent a servant to bring home her little daughter, who had already left the house with the intention of going through the "railway garden," a strip of ground between the sea-wall and the railway-embankment, in order to sit on the great stones by the seaside and see the trains pass by. A few minutes after the little girl's departure, the mother had distinctly and repeatedly heard a voice within her say:

"Send for her back, or something dreadful will happen to her."

Now, soon after, a train ran off the line

and the engine and tender fell, breaking through the protecting wall and crashing down on the very stones where the child was accustomed to sit.

In the other case,[1] into which Professor W. F. Barrett made a special enquiry, Captain MacGowan was in Brooklyn with his two boys, then on their holidays. He promised the boys that he would take them to the theatre and booked seats on the previous day; but on the day of the proposed visit he heard a voice within him constantly saying:

"Do not go to the theatre; take the boys back to school."

He hesitated, gave up his plan and resumed it again. But the words kept repeating themselves and impressing themselves upon him; and, in the end, he definitely decided not to go, much to the two boys' disgust. That night the theatre was de-

[1] *Ibid.*, vol. i., p. 283.

stroyed by fire, with a loss of three hundred lives.

We may add to this the prevision of the Battle of Borodino, to which I have already alluded. I will give the story in fuller detail, as told in the journal of Stephen Grellet the Quaker.

About three months before the French army entered Russia, the wife of General Toutschkoff dreamt that she was at an inn in a town unknown to her and that her father came into her room, holding her only son by the hand, and said to her, in a pitiful tone:

"Your happiness is at an end. He" —meaning Countess Toutschkoff's husband—"has fallen. He has fallen at Borodino."

The dream was repeated a second and a third time. Her anguish of mind was such that she woke her husband and asked him:

"Where is Borodino?"

They looked for the name on the map and did not find it.

Before the French armies reached Moscow, Count Toutschkoff was placed at the head of the army of reserve; and one morning her father, holding her son by the hand, entered her room at the inn where she was staying. In great distress, as she had beheld him in her dream, he cried out:

"He has fallen. He has fallen at Borodino."

Then she saw herself in the very same room and through the windows beheld the very same objects that she had seen in her dreams. Her husband was one of the many who perished in the battle fought near the River Borodino, from which an obscure village takes its name.[1]

23

This is evidently a very rare and perhaps

[1] *Memoirs of the Life and Labours of Stephen Grellet,* vol. i., p. 434.

solitary example of a long-dated prediction of a great historic event which nobody could foresee. It stirs more deeply than any other the enormous problems of fatality, free-will and responsibility. But has it been attested with sufficient rigour for us to rely upon it? That I cannot say. In any case, it has not been sifted by the S.P.R. Next, from the special point of view that interests us for the moment, we are unable to declare that this premonition had any chance of being of avail and preventing the general from going to Borodino. It is highly probable that he did not know where he was going or where he was; besides, the irresistible machinery of war held him fast and it was not his part to disengage his destiny. The premonition, therefore, could only have been given because it was certain not to be obeyed.

As for the two previous cases, nos. clv.

and clviii., we must here again remark the usual strange reservations and observe how difficult it is to explain these premonitions save by attributing them to our subconsciousness. The main, unavoidable event is not precisely stated; but a subordinate consequence seems to be averted, as though to make us believe in some definite power of free-will. Nevertheless, the mysterious entity that foresaw the catastrophe must also have foreseen that nothing would happen to the person whom it was warning; and this brings us back to the useless farce of which we spoke above. Whereas, with the theory of a subconscious self, the latter may have—as in the case of the traveller, the promontory, the copper or the carriage— not this time by inferences or indications that escape our perception, but by other unknown means, a vague presentiment of an impending peril, or, as I have already said, a partial, intermittent and unsettled vision of the future event, and, in its doubt, may utter its cry of alarm.

Whereupon let us recognize that it is almost forbidden to human reason to stray in these regions; and that the part of a prophet is, next to that of a commentator of prophecies, one of the most difficult and thankless that a man can attempt to sustain on the world's stage.

24

I am not sure if it is really necessary, before closing this chapter, to follow in the wake of many others and broach the problem of the preexistence of the future, which includes those of fatality, of free-will, of time and of space, that is to say, all the points that touch the essential sources of the great mystery of the universe. The theologians and the metaphysicians have tackled these problems from every side without giving us the least hope of solving them.

The Unknown Guest

Among those which life sets us, there is none to which our brain seems more definitely and strictly closed; and they remain, if not as unimaginable, at least as incomprehensible as on the day when they were first perceived. What corresponds, outside us, with what we call time and space? We know nothing about it; and Kant, speaking in the name of the "apriorists," who hold that the idea of time is innate in us, does not teach us much when he tells us that time, like space, is an *a priori* form of our sensibility, that is to say, an intuition preceding experience, even as Guyau, among the "empiricists," who consider that this idea is acquired only by experience, does not enlighten us any more by declaring that this same time is the abstract formula of the changes in the universe. Whether space, as Leibnitz maintains, be an order of coexistence and time an order of sequences, whether it be by space that we

succeed in representing time or whether
time be an essential form of any representation, whether time be the father of space
or space the father of time, one thing is
certain, which is that the efforts of the
Kantian or neo-Kantian apriorists and of
the pure empiricists and the idealistic empiricists all end in the same darkness; that
all the philosophers who have grappled
with the formidable dual problem, among
whom one may mention indiscriminately
the names of the greatest thinkers of yesterday and to-day — Herbert Spencer,
Helmholtz, Renouvier, James Sully,
Stumpf, James Ward, William James,
Stuart Mill, Ribot, Fouillée, Guyau, Bain,
Lechalas, Balmès, Dunan and endless
others—have been unable to tame it; and
that, however much their theories may con-
tradict one another, they are all equally
defensible and alike struggle vainly in the

darkness against shadows that are not of our world.

25

To catch a glimpse of this strange problem of the preexistence of the future, as it shows itself to each of us, let us essay more humbly to translate it into tangible images, to place it as it were upon the stage. I am writing these lines sitting on a stone, in the shade of some tall beeches that overlook a little Norman village. It is one of those lovely summer days when the sweetness of life is almost visible in the azure vase of earth and sky. In the distance stretches the immense, fertile valley of the Seine, with its green meadows planted with restful trees, between which the river flows like a long path of gladness leading to the misty hills of the estuary. I am looking down on the village-square, with its ring of young lime-trees. A procession leaves the church and, amid prayers and chanting, they carry the statue of the Virgin around the sacred pile. I am conscious of all the details of the ceremony: the sly old curé perfunctorily bearing a small reliquary; four choirmen opening their mouths to bawl forth vacantly the Latin words which convey nothing to them; two mischievous serving-boys in frayed cassocks; a score of little girls, young girls and old maids in white, all starched and flounced, followed by six or seven .village notables in baggy frockcoats. The pageant disappears behind the trees, comes into sight again at the bend of the road and hurries back into the church. The clock in the steeple strikes five, as though to ring down the curtain and mark in the infinite history of events which none will recollect the conclusion of a spectacle which never again, until the end of the world and of the universe of worlds, will be just what it was during those seconds when it beguiled my wandering eyes.

The Unknown Guest

For in vain will they repeat the procession next year and every year after: never again will it be the same. Not only will several of the actors probably have disappeared, but all those who resume their old places in the ranks will have undergone the thousand little visible and invisible changes wrought by the passing days and weeks. In a word, this insignificant moment is unique, irrecoverable, inimitable, as are all the moments in the existence of all things; and this little picture, enduring for a few seconds suspended in boundless duration, has lapsed into eternity, where henceforth it will remain in its entirety to the end of time, so much so that, if a man could one day recapture in the past, among what some one has called the "astral negatives," the image of what it was, he would find it intact, unchanged, ineffaceable and undeniable.

It is not difficult for us to conceive that one can thus go back and see again the astral negative of an event that is no more; and retrospective clairvoyance appears to us a wonderful but not an impossible thing. It astonishes but does not stagger our reason. But, when it becomes a question of discovering the same picture in the future, the boldest imagination flounders at the first step. How are we to admit that there exists somewhere a representation or reproduction of that which has not yet existed? Nevertheless, some of the incidents which we have just been considering seem to prove in an almost conclusive manner not only that such representations are possible, but that we may arrive at them more frequently, not to say more conveniently, than at those of the past. Now, once this representation preexists, as we are obliged to admit in the case of a certain number of premonitions, the riddle remains the same whether the preexistence be one of a few hours, a few years or several centuries. It is therefore possible—for, in these matters, we must go straight to extremes or else leave them alone—it is therefore possible that a seer mightier than any of to-day, some god, demigod or demon, some unknown, universal or vagrant intelligence, saw that procession a million years ago, at a time when nothing existed of that which composes and surrounds it and when the very earth on which it moves had not yet risen from the ocean depths. And other seers, as mighty as the first, who from age to age contemplated the same spot and the same moment, would always have perceived, through the vicissitudes and upheavals of seas, shores and forests, the same procession going round the same little church that still lay slumbering in the oceanic ooze and made up of the same per-

sons sprung from a race that was perhaps
not yet represented on the earth.

27

It is obviously difficult for us to understand that the future can thus precede
chaos, that the present is at the same time
the future and the past, or that that which
is not yet exists already at the same time
at which it is no more. But, on the other
hand, it is just as hard to conceive that
the future does not preexist, that there is
nothing before the present and that everything is only present or past. It is very
probable that, to a more universal intelligence than ours, everything is but an eternal present, an immense *punctum stans,* as
the metaphysicians say, in which all the
events are on one plane; but it is no less
probable that we ourselves, so long as we
are men, in order to understand anything of
this eternal present, will always be obliged

to divide it into three parts. Thus caught between two mysteries equally baffling to our intelligence, whether we deny or admit the preexistence of the future, we are really only wrangling over words: in the one case, we give the name of "present," from the point of view of a perfect intelligence, to that which to us is the future; in the other, we give the name of "future" to that which, from the point of view of a perfect intelligence, is the present. But, after all, it is incontestable in both cases that, at least from our point of view, the future preexists, since preexistence is the only name by which we can describe and the only form under which we can conceive that which we do not yet see in the present.

28

Attempts have been made to shed light on the riddle by transferring it to space. It is true that it there loses the greater part of its obscurity; but this apparently is because, in changing its environment, it has completely changed its nature and no longer bears any relation to what it was when it was placed in time. We are told, for instance, that innumerable cities distributed over the surface of the earth are to us as if they were not, so long as we have not seen them, and only begin to exist on the day when we visit them. That is true; but space, outside all metaphysical speculations, has realities for us which time does not possess. Space, although very mysterious and incomprehensible once we pass certain limits, is nevertheless not, like time, incomprehensible and illusory in all its parts. We are certainly quite able to conceive that those towns which we have never seen and doubtless never will see indubitably exist, whereas we find it much more difficult to imagine that the catastrophe which, fifty years hence, will annihi-

late one of them already exists as really as
the town itself. We are capable of pic-
turing a spot whence, with keener eyes than
those which we boast to-day, we should see
in one glance all the cities of the earth and
even those of other worlds, but it is much
less easy for us to imagine a point in the
ages whence we should simultaneously discover the past, the present and the future,
because the past, the present and the future
are three orders of duration which cannot
find room at the same time in our intelligence and which inevitably devour one another. How can we picture to ourselves,
for instance, a point in eternity at which
our little procession already exists, while it
is not yet and although it is no more? Add
to this the thought that it is necessary and
inevitable, from the millenaries which had
no beginning, that, at a given moment, at
a given place, the little procession should
leave the little church in a given manner

and that no known or imaginable will can change anything in it, in the future any more than in the past; and we begin to understand that there is no hope of understanding.

29

We find among the cases collected by M. Bozzano a singular premonition wherein the unknown factors of space and time are continued in a very curious fashion. In August, 1910, Cavaliere Giovanni de Figueroa, one of the most famous fencing-masters at Palermo, dreamt that he was in the country, going along a road white with dust, which brought him to a broad ploughed field. In the middle of the field stood a rustic building, with a ground-floor used for store-rooms and cow-sheds and on the right a rough hut made of branches and a cart with some harness lying in it.

A peasant wearing dark trousers, with a

black felt hat on his head, came forward to
meet him, asked him to follow him and took
him round behind the house. Through a
low, narrow door they entered a little stable
with a short, winding stone staircase leading to a loft over the entrance to the house.
A mule fastened to a swinging manger was
blocking the bottom step; and the chevalier
had to push it aside before climbing the
staircase. On reaching the loft, he noticed
that from the ceiling were suspended strings
of melons, tomatoes, onions and Indian
corn. In this room were two women and a
little girl; and through a door leading to
another room he caught sight of an extremely high bed, unlike any that he had ever seen
before.

Here the dream broke off. It seemed to
him so strange that he spoke of it to several
of his friends, whom he mentions by name
and who are ready to confirm his statements.

The Unknown Guest

On the 12th of October in the same year, in order to support a fellow-townsman in a duel, he accompanied the seconds, by motor-car, from Naples to Marano, a place which he had never visited nor even heard of. As soon as they were some way in the country, he was curiously impressed by the white and dusty road. The car pulled up at the side of a field which he at once recognized. They alighted; and he remarked to one of the seconds:

"This is not the first time that I have been here. There should be a house at the end of this path and on the right a hut and a cart with some harness in it."

As a matter of fact, everything was as he described it. An instant later, at the exact moment foreseen by the dream, the peasant in the dark trousers and the black felt hat came up and asked him to follow him. But, instead of walking behind him, the chevalier went in front, for he already knew the way.

He found the stable and, exactly at the
place which it occupied two months before,
near its swinging manger, the mule blocking
the way to the staircase. The fencing-
master went up the steps and once more saw
the loft, with the ceiling hung with melons,
onions and tomatoes, and, in a corner on the
right, the two silent women and the child,
identical with the figures in his dream, while
in the next room he recognized the bed
whose extraordinary height had so much
impressed him.

It really looks as if the facts themselves,
the extramundane realities, the eternal verities, or whatever we may be pleased to call
them, have tried to show us here that time
and space are one and the same illusion, one
and the same convention and have no existence outside our little day-spanned understanding; that "everywhere" and "always"
are exactly synonymous terms and reign
alone as soon as we cross the narrow

boundaries of the obscure consciousness in which we live. We are quite ready to admit that Cavaliere de Figueroa may have had by clairvoyance an exact and detailed vision of places which he was not to visit until later: this is a pretty frequent and almost classical phenomenon, which, as it affects the realities of space, does not astonish us beyond measure and, in any case, does not take us out of the world which our senses perceive. The field, the house, the hut, the loft do not move; and it is no miracle that they should be found in the same place. But, suddenly, quitting this domain where all is stationary, the phenomenon is transferred to time and, in those unknown places, at the foretold second, brings together all the moving actors of that little drama in two acts, of which the first was performed some two and a half months before, in the depths of some mysterious other life where it seemed to be motionlessly and irrevocably awaiting its terrestrial realization. Any explanation would but condense this vapour of petty mysteries into a few drops in the ocean of mysteries.

Let us note here again, in passing, the strange freakishness of these premonitions. They accumulate the most precise and circumstantial details as long as the scene remains insignificant, but come to a sudden stop before the one tragic and interesting scene of the drama: the duel and its issue. Here again we recognize the inconsistent, impotent, ironical or humorous habits of our unknown guest.

30

But we will not prolong these somewhat vain speculations concerning space and time. We are merely playing with words that represent very badly ideas which we do not put into form at all. To sum up, if it is difficult for us to conceive that the future preexists, perhaps it is even more difficult for us to understand that it does not exist; moreover, a certain number of facts tend to prove that it is as real and definite and has, both in time and in eternity, the same permanence and the same vividness as the past. Now, from the moment that it preexists, it is not surprising that we should be able to know it; it is even astonishing, granted that it overhangs us on every side, that we should not discover it oftener and more easily. It remains to be learnt what would become of our life if everything were foreseen in it, if we saw it unfolding beforehand, in its entirety, with its events which would have to be inevitable, because, if it were possible for us to avoid them, they would not exist and we could not perceive them. Suppose that, instead of being abnormal, uncertain, obscure, debatable and very unusual, prediction became, so to speak, scientific, habitual, clear and infallible: in a short time, having nothing more to foretell, it would die of inanition. If, for instance, it was prophesied to me that I must die in the course of a journey in Italy, I should naturally abandon the journey; therefore it could not have been predicted to me; and thus all life would soon be nothing but inaction, pause and abstention, a sort of vast desert where the embryos of still-born events would be gathered in heaps and where nothing would grow save perhaps one or two more or less fortunate enterprises and the little insignificant incidents which no one would trouble to avoid. But these again are questions to which there is no solution; and we will not pursue them further.

CHAPTER IV
THE ELBERFELD HORSES

CHAPTER IV

THE ELBERFELD HORSES

I

I WILL first sum up as briefly as possible, for whoso may still be ignorant of them, the facts which it is necessary to know if one would fully understand the marvellous story of the Elberfeld horses. For a detailed account, I can refer him to Herr Karl Krall's remarkable work, *Denkende Tiere* (Leipsic, 1912), which is the first and principal source of information amid a bibliography that is already assuming considerable dimensions.

Some twenty years ago there lived in Berlin an old misanthrope named Wilhelm von Osten. He was a man with a small private income, a little eccentric in his ways and obsessed by one idea, the intelligence of animals. He began by undertaking the education of a horse that gave him no very definite results. But, in 1900, he became the owner of a Russian stallion who, under the name of *Hans,* to which was soon added the Homeric and well-earned prefix of *Kluge,* or Clever, was destined to upset all our notions of animal psychology and to raise questions that rank among the most unexpected and the most absorbing problems which man has yet encountered.

Thanks to Von Osten, whose patience, contrary to what one might think, was in no wise angelic but resembled rather a frenzied obstinacy, the horse made rapid and extraordinary progress. This progress is very aptly described by Professor E. Clarapède, of the university of Geneva, who says, in his excellent monograph on the Elberfeld horses:

"After making him familiar with various common ideas, such as right, left, top, bottom and so on, his master began to teach him arithmetic by the intuitive method. Hans was brought to a table on which were placed first one, then two, then several small skittles. Von Osten, kneeling beside Hans, uttered the corresponding numbers, at the same time making him strike as many blows with his hoof as there were skittles on the table. Before long, the skittles were replaced by figures written on a blackboard. The results were astonishing. The horse was capable not only of counting (that is to say, of striking as many blows as he was asked), but also of himself making real calculations, of solving little problems. . . .

"But Hans could do more than mere sums: he knew how to read; he was a musician, distinguishing between harmonious and dissonant chords. He also had an extraordinary memory: he could tell the date of each day of the current week. In short, he got through all the tasks which an intelligent schoolboy of fourteen is able to perform."

2

The rumour of these curious experiments soon spread; and visitors flocked to the little stable-yard in which Von Osten kept his singular pupil at work. The newspapers took the matter up; and a fierce controversy broke forth between those who believed in the genuineness of the phenomenon and those who saw no more in it than a barefaced fraud. A scientific committee was appointed in 1904, consisting of professors of psychology and physiology, of the director of a zoological garden, of a circus-manager and of veterinary surgeons and cavalry-officers. The committee discovered nothing suspicious, but ventured upon no explanation. A second committee was then appointed, numbering among its members Herr Oskar Pfungst, of the Berlin psychological laboratory. Herr Pfungst, after a

long series of experiments, drew up a voluminous and crushing report, in which he
maintained that the horse was gifted with
no intelligence, that it did not recognize
either letters or figures, that it really knew
neither how to calculate nor how to count,
but merely obeyed the imperceptible, infinitesimal and unconscious signs which
escaped from its master.

Public opinion veered round suddenly
and completely. People felt a sort of half-
cowardly relief at beholding the prompt
collapse of a miracle which was threatening
to throw confusion into the self-satisfied
little fold of established truths. Poor Von
Osten protested in vain: no one listened to
him; the verdict was given. He never re-
covered from this official blow; he became
the laughing-stock of all those whom he had
at first astounded; and he died, lonely and
embittered, on the 29th of June, 1909, at
the age of seventy-one.

3

But he left a disciple whose faith had not been shaken by the general defection. A well-to-do Elberfeld manufacturer, Herr Krall, had taken a great interest in Von Osten's labours and, during the latter years of the old man's life, had eagerly followed and even on occasion directed the education of the wonderful stallion. Von Osten left Kluge Hans to him by will; on his own side, Krall had bought two Arab stallions, *Muhamed* and *Zarif,* whose prowess soon surpassed that of the pioneer. The whole question was reopened, events took a vigorous and decisive turn and, instead of a weary, eccentric old man, discouraged almost to sullenness and with no weapons for the struggle, the critics of the miracle found themselves faced by a new adversary, young and high-spirited, endowed with remarkable scientific instinct, quick-witted, scholarly and well able to defend himself.

The Unknown Guest

His educational methods also differ materially from Von Osten's. It was a strange thing, but deep down in the rather queer, cross-grained soul of the old enthusiast there had grown up gradually a sort of hatred for his four-legged pupil. He felt the stallion's proud and nervous will resisting his with an obstinacy which he qualified as diabolical. They stood up to each other like two enemies; and the lessons almost assumed the form of a tragic and secret struggle in which the animal's soul rebelled against man's domination.

Krall, on the other hand, adores his pupils; and this atmosphere of affection has in a manner of speaking humanized them. There are no longer those sudden movements of wild panic which reveal the ancestral dread of man in the quietest and best-trained horse. He talks to them long and tenderly, as a father might talk to his children; and we have the strange feeling that they listen to all that he says and understand it. If they appear not to grasp an explanation or a demonstration, he will begin it all over again, analyze it, paraphrase it ten times in succession, with the patience of a mother. And so their progress has been incomparably swifter and more astounding than that of old Hans. Within a fortnight of the first lesson, Muhamed did simple little addition- and subtraction-sums quite correctly. He had learnt to distinguish the tens from the units, striking the latter with his right foot and the former with his left. He knew the meaning of the symbols plus and minus. Four days later, he was beginning multiplication and division. In four months' time, he knew how to extract square and cubic roots; and, soon after, he learnt to spell and read by means of the conventional alphabet devised by Krall.

This alphabet, at the first glance, seems rather complicated. For that matter, it is only a makeshift; but how could one find anything better? The unfortunate horse, who is almost voiceless, has only one way in which to express himself: a clumsy hoof, which was not created to put thought into words. It became necessary, therefore, to contrive, as in table-turning, a special alphabet, in which each letter is designated by a certain number of blows struck by the right foot and the left. Here is the copy handed to visitors at Elberfeld to enable them to follow the horse's operations:

	I	2	3	4	5	6
10	E	N	R	S	M	C
20	A	H	L	T	Ä	CH
30	I	D	G	W	J	SCH
40	O	B	F	K	Ö	
50	U	V	Z	P	Ü	
60	EI	AU	EU	X	Q	

To mark the letter E, for instance, the stallion will strike one blow with his left foot and one with his right; for the letter L, two blows with his left foot and three with his right; and so on. The horses have this alphabet so deeply imprinted in their memory that, practically speaking, they never make a mistake; and they strike their hoofs so quickly, one after the other, that at first one has some difficulty in following them.

Muhamed and Zarif—for Zarif's progress was almost equal to that of his fellow-pupil, though he seems a little less gifted from the standpoint of higher mathematics—Muhamed and Zarif in this way reproduce the words spoken in their presence, spell the names of their visitors, reply to questions put to them and sometimes make little observations, little personal and spontaneous reflections to which we shall return presently. They have created for their own use an inconceivably fantastic and phonetic system of spelling which they stubbornly refuse to relinquish and which often makes their writing rather difficult to read. Deeming most of the vowels useless, they keep almost exclusively to the consonants; thus *Zucker*, for instance, becomes Z K R, *Pferd*, P F R T or F R T, and so on.

I will not set forth in detail the many different proofs of intelligence lavished by the singular inhabitants of this strange stable. They are not only first-class calculators, for whom the most repellent fractions and roots possess hardly any secrets: they distinguish sounds, colours, and scents, read the time on the face of a watch, recognize certain geometrical figures, likenesses and photographs.

Following on these more and more conclusive experiments and especially after the publication of Krall's great work, *Denkende Tiere*, a model of precision and arrangement, men's minds were faced with a clear and definite problem which, this time, could not be challenged. Scientific committees followed one another at Elberfeld; and their reports became legion. Learned men of every country—including Dr. Edinger, the eminent Frankfort neurologist; Professors Dr. H. Kraemer and H. E. Ziegler, of Stuttgart; Dr. Paul Sarasin, of Bâle; Professor Ostwald, of Berlin; Professor A. Beredka, of the Pasteur Institute; Dr. E. Clarapède, of the university of Geneva; Professor Schoeller and Professor Gehrke, the natural philosopher, of Berlin; Professor Goldstein, of Darmstadt; Professor von Buttel-Reepen, of Oldenburg; Professor William Mackenzie, of Genoa; Professor R. Assagioli, of Florence; Dr. Hartkopf, of Cologne; Dr. Freudenberg, of Brussels; Dr. Ferrari, of Bologna, etc., etc., for the list is lengthening daily—came to study on the spot the inexplicable phenomenon which Dr. Clarapède proclaims to be "the most sensational event that has ever happened in the psychological world."

With the exception of two or three sceptics or convinced misoneists and of those who made too short a stay at Elberfeld, all were unanimous in recognizing that the facts were as stated and that the experiments were conducted with absolute fairness. Disagreement begins only when it becomes a matter of commenting on them, interpreting them and explaining them.

4

To complete this short preamble, it is right to add that, for some time past, the case of the Elberfeld horses no longer stands quite alone. There exists at Mannheim a dog of a rather doubtful breed who performs almost the same feats as his equine rivals. He is less advanced than they in arithmetic, but does little additions, subtractions and multiplications of one or two figures correctly. He reads and writes by tapping with his paw, in accordance with an alphabet which, it appears, he has thought out for himself; and his spelling also is simplified and phoneticized to the utmost. He distinguishes the colours in a bunch of flowers, counts the money in a purse and separates the marks from the pfennigs. He knows how to seek and find words to define the object or the picture placed before him. You show him, for instance, a bouquet in a vase and ask him what it is.

"A glass with little flowers," he replies.

And his answers are often curiously spontaneous and original. In the course of a reading-exercise in which the word *Herbst,* autumn, chanced to attract attention, Professor William Mackenzie asked him if he could explain what autumn was.

"It is the time when there are apples," Rolf replied.

On the same occasion, the same professor, without knowing what it represented, held out to him a card marked with red and blue squares:

"What's this?"

"Blue, red, lots of cubes," replied the dog.

Sometimes his repartees are not lacking in humour.

"Is there anything you would like me to do for you?" a lady of his acquaintance asked, one day.

And Master Rolf gravely answered:

"Wedelen," which means, "Wag your tail!"

Rolf, whose fame is comparatively young, has not yet, like his illustrious rivals of the Rhine Province, been the object of minute enquiries and copious and innumerable reports. But the incidents which I have just mentioned and which are vouched for by such men as Professor Mackenzie and M. Duchatel, the learned and clear-sighted vice-president of the Société Universelle d'Etudes Psychiques,[1] who went to Mannheim for the express purpose of studying them, appear to be no more controvertible than the Elberfeld occurrences, of which they are a sort of replica or echo. It is not unusual to find these coincidences amongst abnormal phenomena. They spring up simultaneously in different quarters of the globe, correspond with one another and multiply as though in obedience to a word of command. It is probable therefore that we shall see still more manifestations of the same class. One might almost say that a new spirit is passing over the world and, after awakening in man forces whereof he was not aware, is now reaching other creatures who with us inhabit this mysterious earth, on which they live, suffer and die, as we do, without knowing why.

[1] See the interesting lecture by M. Edmond Duchatel, published in the *Annales des sciences psychiques*, October 1913.

The Unknown Guest

5

I have not been to Mannheim, but I made my pilgrimage to Elberfeld and stayed long enough in the town to carry away with me the conviction shared by all those who have undertaken the journey.

A few months ago, Herr Krall, whom I had promised the year before that I would come and see his wonderful horses, was kind enough to repeat his invitation in a more pressing fashion, adding that his stable would perhaps be broken up after the 15th of September and that, in any case, he would be obliged, by his doctor's orders, to interrupt for an indefinite period a course of training which he found exceedingly fatiguing.

I at once left for Elberfeld, which, as everybody knows, is an important manufacturing-town in Rhenish Prussia and is, in fact, more quaint, pleasing and picturesque than one might expect. I had long since read everything that had been published on the question; and I was wholly persuaded of the genuineness of the incidents. Indeed it would be difficult to have any doubts after the repeated and unremitting supervision and verification to which the experiments are subjected, a supervision which is of the most rigorous type, often hostile and almost ill-mannered. As for their interpretation, I was convinced that telepathy, that is to say, the transmission of thought from one subconsciousness to another, remained, however strange it might be in this new region, the only acceptable theory; and this in spite of certain circumstances that seemed plainly to exclude it. In default of telepathy proper, I inclined towards the mediumistic or subliminal theory, which was very ably outlined by M. de Vesmes in a remarkable lecture delivered, on the 22nd of December, 1912, before the Société Universelle d'Études Psychiques.

It is true that telepathy, especially when carried to its extreme limits, appeals above all to the subliminal forces, so that the two theories overlap at more than one point and it is often difficult to make out where the first ends and the second begins. But this discussion will be more appropriate a little later.

6

I found Herr Krall in his goldsmith's-shop, a sort of palace of Golconda, streaming and glittering with the most precious pearls and stones on earth. Herr Krall, it is well to remember, in order to dispel any suspicion of pecuniary interest, is a rich manufacturer whose family for three generations, from father to son, have conducted one of the most important jewellery-businesses in Germany. His researches, so far from bringing him the least profit, cost him a great deal of money, take up all his leisure and some part of the time which he would otherwise devote to his business and, as usually happens, procure him from his fellow-citizens and from not a few scientific men more annoyance, unfair criticism and sarcasm than consideration or gratitude. His work is preeminently the disinterested and thankless task of the apostle and pioneer.

For the rest, Herr Krall, though his faith is active, zealous and infectious, has nothing in common with the visionaries or illuminati. He is a man of about fifty, vigorous, alert and enthusiastic, but at the same time well-balanced; accessible to every idea and even to every dream, yet practical and methodical, with a ballast of the most invincible common-sense. He inspires from the outset that fine confidence, frank and unrestrained, which instantly disperses the instinctive doubt, the strange uneasiness and the veiled suspicion that generally separate two people who meet for the first time; and one welcomes in him, from the very depths of one's being, the honest man, the staunch friend whom one can trust and whom one is sorry not to have known earlier in life.

We go together through the streets and along the bustling quays of Elberfeld to the stable, situated at a few hundred steps from the shop. The horses are taking the air outside the doors of their boxes, in the yard shaded by a lime-tree. There are four of them: Muhamed, the most intelligent, the most gifted of them all, the great mathematician of the party; his double, Zarif, a little less advanced, less tractable, craftier, but at the same time more fanciful, more spontaneous and capable of occasional disconcerting sallies; next, *Hänschen,* a little Shetland pony, hardly bigger than a Newfoundland dog, the street-urchin of the band, always quivering with excitement, roguish, flighty, uncertain and passionate, but ready in a moment to work you out the most difficult addition- and multiplication-sums with a furious scrape of the hoof; and lastly the latest arrival, the plump and placid *Berto,* an imposing black stallion, quite blind and lacking the sense of smell. He has been only a few months at school and is still, so to speak, in the preparatory class, but already does—a little more clumsily, but more good-humouredly and conscientiously—small addition- and subtraction-sums quite as well as many a child of the same age.

In a corner, *Kama,* a young elephant two or three years old, about the size of an outrageously "blown" donkey, rolls his mischievous and almost knavish eyes under the shelter of his wide ears, each resembling a great rhubarb-leaf, and with his stealthy, insinuating trunk carefully picks up whatever he considers fit to eat, that is to say, pretty well everything that lies about on the stones. Great things were hoped of him, but hitherto he has disappointed all expectations: he is the dunce of the establishment. Perhaps he is too young still: his little elephant-soul no doubt resembles that of a sucking-babe which, in the place of its feet and hands, plays with the stupendous nose that must first explore and question the universe. It is impossible to grip his attention; and, when they set out before him his alphabet of movable letters, instead of naming those which are pointed out to him he applies himself to pulling them off their stems, in order to swallow them surreptitiously. He has disheartened his kind master, who, pending the coming of the reason and wisdom promised by the proboscidian legends, leaves him in a contented state of ignorance made more blissful by an almost insatiable appetite.

7

But I ask to see the great pioneer, Kluge Hans, Clever Hans. He is still alive. He is old: he must be sixteen or seventeen; but his old age, alas, is not exempt from the baneful troubles from which men themselves suffer in their decline! Hans has turned out badly, it appears, and is never mentioned save in ambiguous terms. An imprudent or vindictive groom, I forget which, having introduced a mare into the yard, Hans the Pure, who till then had led an austere and monkish existence, vowed to celibacy, science and the chaste delights of figures, Hans the Irreproachable incontinently lost his head and cut himself open on the hanging-rail of his stall. They had to force back his intestines and sew up his belly. He is now rusticating miserably in a meadow outside the town. So true it is that a life cannot be judged except at its close and that we are sure of nothing until we are dead.

8

Before the sitting begins, while the

master is making his morning inspection, I
go up to Muhamed, speak to him and pat
him, looking straight into his eyes meanwhile in order to catch a sign of his genius.
The handsome creature, well-bred and in
hard condition, is as calm and trusting as
a dog; he shows himself excessively gra-
cious and friendly and tries to give me some
huge licks and mighty kisses which I do my
best to avoid because they are a little unexpected and overdemonstrative. The expression of his limpid antelope-eyes is deep,
serious and remote, but it differs in no wise
from that of his brothers who, for thousands of years, have seen nothing but
brutality and ingratitude in man. If we
were able to read anything there, it would
not be that insufficient and vain little effort
which we call thought, but rather an indefinable, vast anxiety, a tear-dimmed regret
for the boundless, stream-crossed plains
where his sires sported at will before they

knew man's yoke. In any case, to see him thus fastened by a halter to the stable-door, beating off the flies and absently pawing the cobbles, Muhamed is nothing more than a well-trained horse who seems to be waiting for his saddle or harness and who hides his new secret as profoundly as all the others which nature has buried in him.

9

But they are summoning me to take my place in the stable where the lessons are given. It is a small room, empty and bare, with peat-moss litter bedding and white-washed walls. The horse is separated from the people present by breast-high wooden partitions. Opposite the four-legged scholar is a black-board, nailed to the wall; and on one side a corn-bin which forms a seat for the spectators. Muhamed is led in. Krall, who is a little nervous, makes no secret of his uneasiness. His horses are fickle animals, uncertain, capricious and extremely sensitive. A trifle disturbs them, confuses them, puts them off. At such times, threats, prayers and even the irresistible charm of carrots and good rye-bread are useless. They obstinately refuse to do any work and they answer at random. Everything depends on a whim, the state of the weather, the morning meal or the impression which the visitor makes upon them. Still, Krall seems to know, by certain imperceptible signs, that this is not going to be a bad day. Muhamed quivers with excitement, snorts loudly through his nostrils, utters a series of indistinct little whinnyings: excellent symptoms, it appears. I take my seat on the corn-bin. The master, standing beside the black-board, chalk in hand, introduces me to Muhamed in due form, as to a human being:

"Muhamed, attention! This is your uncle"—pointing to me—"who has come

all the way to honour you with a visit.
Mind you don't disappoint him. His name
is Maeterlinck." Krall pronounces the
first syllable German-fashion: *Mah*. "You
understand: Maeterlinck. Now show him
that you know your letters and that you can
spell a name correctly, like a clever boy.
Go ahead, we're listening."

Muhamed gives a short neigh and, on
the small, movable board at his feet, strikes
first with his right hoof and then with his
left the number of blows which correspond
with the letter M in the conventional alphabet used by the horses. Then, one after
the other, without stopping or hesitating, he
marks the letters A D R L I N S H, representing the unexpected aspect which my
humble name assumes in the equine mind
and phonetics. His attention is called to
the fact that there is a mistake. He readily agrees and replaces the S H by a G
and then the G by a K. They insist that

he must put a T instead of the D; but Muhamed, content with his work, shakes his head to say no and refuses to make any further corrections.

10

I assure you that the first shock is rather disturbing, however much one expected it. I am quite aware that, when one describes these things, one is taken for a dupe too readily dazzled by the doubtless childish illusion of an ingeniously-contrived scene. But what contrivances, what illusions have we here? Do they lie in the spoken word? Why, to admit that the horse understands and translates his master's words is just to accept the most extraordinary part of the phenomenon! Is it a case of surreptitious touches or conventional signs? However simple-minded one may be, one would nevertheless notice them more easily than a horse, even a horse of genius. Krall never lays a hand on the animal; he moves all round the little stable, which contains no appliances of any sort; for the most part, he stands behind the horse, which is unable to see him, or comes and sits beside his guest on the innocuous corn-bin, busying himself, while lecturing his pupil, in writing up the minutes of the lesson. He also welcomes with the most serene readiness any restrictions or tests which you propose. I assure you that the thing itself is much simpler and clearer than the suspicions of the arm-chair critics and that the most distrustful mind would not entertain the faintest idea of fraud in the frank, wholesome atmosphere of the old stable.

"But," some one might have said, "Krall, who knew that you were coming to Elberfeld, had of course thoroughly rehearsed his little exercise in spelling, which apparently is only an exercise in memory."

For conscience' sake, though I did not

look upon the objection as serious, I submitted it to Krall, who at once said:

"Try it for yourself. Dictate to the
horse any German word of two or three
syllables, emphasizing it strongly. I'll go
out of the stable and leave you alone with
him."

Behold Muhamed and me by ourselves.
I confess that I am a little frightened. I
have many a time felt less uncomfortable in
the presence of the great ones or the kings
of the earth. Whom am I dealing with
exactly? However, I summon my courage
and speak aloud the first word that occurs
to me, the name of the hotel at which I am
staying: Weidenhof. At first, Muhamed,
who seems a little puzzled by his master's
absence, appears not to hear me and does
not even deign to notice that I am there.
But I repeat eagerly, in varying tones of
voice, by turns insinuating, threatening, be-
seeching and commanding:

"Weidenhof! Weidenhof! Weidenhof!"

At last, my mysterious companion suddenly makes up his mind to lend me his ears and straightway blithely raps out the following letters, which I write down on the black-board as they come:

WEIDNHOZ.

It is a magnificent specimen of equine spelling! Triumphant and bewildered, I call in friend Krall, who, accustomed as he is to the prodigy, thinks it quite natural, but knits his brows:

"What's this, Muhamed? You've made a mistake again. It's an F you want at the end of the word, not a Z. Just correct it at once, please."

And the docile Muhamed, recognizing his blunder, gives the three blows with his right hoof, followed by the four blows with his left, which represent the most unexceptionable F that one could ask for.

Observe, by the way, the logic of his phonetic writing: contrary to his habit, he strikes the mute E after the W, because it is indispensable; but, finding it included in the D, he considers it superfluous and suppresses it with a high hand.

You rub your eyes, question yourself, ask yourself in the presence of what humanized phenomenon, of what unknown force, of what new creature you stand. Was all this what they hid in their eyes, those silent brothers of ours? You blush at man's long injustice. You look around you for some sort of trace, obvious or subtle, of the mystery. You feel yourself attacked in your innermost citadel, where you held yourself most certain and most impregnable. You have felt a breath from the abyss upon your face. You would not be more astonished if you suddenly heard the voice of the dead.

But the most astonishing thing is that you are not astonished for long. We all, unknown to ourselves, live in the expectation of the extraordinary; and, when it comes, it moves us much less than did the expectation. It is as though a sort of higher instinct, which knows everything and is not ignorant of the miracles that hang over our heads, were reassuring us in advance and helping us to make an easy entrance into the regions of the supernatural. There is nothing to which we grow accustomed more readily than to the marvellous; and it is only afterwards, upon reflection, that our intelligence, which knows hardly anything, appreciates the magnitude of certain phenomena.

II

But Muhamed gives unmistakable signs of impatience to show that he has had enough of spelling. Thereupon, as a diversion and a reward, his kind master suggests the extraction of a few square and cubic roots. Muhamed appears delighted: these are his favourite problems; for he takes less interest than formerly in the most difficult multiplications and divisions. He doubtless thinks them beneath him.

Krall therefore writes on the blackboard various numbers of which I did not take note. Moreover, as nobody now contests the fact that the horse works them with ease, it would hardly be interesting to reproduce here several rather grim problems of which numerous variants will be found in the accounts and reports of experiments signed by Drs. Mackenzie and Hartkopff, by Overbeck, Clarapède and many others. What strikes one particularly is the facility, the quickness, I was almost saying the joyous carelessness with which the strange mathematician gives the answers. The last figure is hardly chalked upon the board before the right hoof is striking off the units, followed immediately by the left hoof marking the tens. There is not a sign of attention or reflection; one is not even aware of the exact moment at which the horse looks at the problem; and the answer seems to spring automatically from an invisible intelligence. Mistakes are rare or frequent according as it happens to be a good or bad day with the horse; but, when he is told of them, he nearly always corrects them. Not unseldom, the number is reversed: 47, for instance, becomes 74; but he puts it right without demur when asked.

I am manifestly dumbfounded; but perhaps these problems are prepared beforehand? If they were, it would be very extraordinary, but yet less surprising than their actual solution. Krall does not read this suspicion in my eyes, because they do not show it; nevertheless, to remove the least shade of it, he asks me to write a

number of my own on the black-board for
the horse to find the root.

I must here confess the humiliating ignorance that is the disgrace of my life. I
have not the faintest idea of the mysteries
concealed within those recondite and complicated operations. I did my humanities
like everybody else; but, after crossing the
useful and familiar frontiers of multiplication and division I found it impossible to
advance any farther into the desolate regions, bristling with figures, where the
square and cubic roots hold sway, together
with all sorts of other monstrous powers,
without shapes or faces, which inspired me
with invincible terror. All the persecutions
of my excellent instructors wore themselves
out against a dead wall of stolidity. Suc-
cessively disheartened, they left me to my
dismal ignorance, prophesying a most dreary
future for me, haunted with bitter regrets.
I must say that, until now, I had scarcely

experienced the effects of these gloomy predictions; but the hour has come for me to expiate the sins of my youth. Nevertheless, I put a good face upon it; and, taking at random the first figures that suggest themselves to my mind, I boldly write on the black-board an enormous and most daring number. Muhamed remains motionless. Krall speaks to him sharply, telling him to hurry up. Muhamed lifts his right hoof, but does not let it fall. Krall loses patience, lavishes prayers, promises and threats; the hoof remains poised, as though to bear witness to good intentions that cannot be carried out. Then my host turns round, looks at the problem and asks me:

"Does it give an exact root?"

Exact? What does he mean? Are there roots which . . . ? But I dare not go on: my shameful ignorance suddenly flashes before my eyes. Krall smiles indulgently and, without making any attempt to supplement an education which is too much in arrears to allow of the slightest hope, laboriously works out the problem and declares that the horse was right in refusing to give an impossible solution.

12

Muhamed receives our thanks in the form of a lordly portion of carrots; and a pupil is introduced whose attainments do not tower so high above mine: Hänschen, the little pony, quick and lively as a big rat. Like me, he has never gone beyond elementary arithmetic; and so we shall understand each other better and meet on equal terms.

Krall asks me for two numbers to multiply. I give him 63×7. He does the sum and writes the product on the board, followed by the sign of division: $441 \div 7$. Instantly Hänschen, with a celerity difficult to follow, gives three blows, or rather three violent scrapes with his right hoof and six with his left, which makes 63, for we must not forget that in German they say not sixty-three, but three-and-sixty. We congratulate him; and, to evince his satisfaction, he nimbly reverses the number by marking 36 and then puts it right again by scraping 63. He is evidently enjoying himself and juggling with the figures. And additions, subtractions, multiplications and divisions follow one after the other, with figures supplied by myself, so as to remove any idea of collusion. Hänschen seldom blunders; and, when he does, we receive a very clear impression that his mistake is voluntary: he is like a mischievous schoolboy playing a practical joke upon his master. The solutions fall thick as hail upon the little spring-board; the correct answer is released by the question as though you were pressing the button of an electric push. The pony's flippancy is as surprising as his skill. But in this unruly flippancy, in this hastiness which seems inattentive there is nevertheless a fixed and permanent idea. Hänschen paws the ground, kicks, prances, tosses his head, looks as if he cannot keep still, but never leaves his spring-board. Is he interested in the problems, does he enjoy them? It is impossible to say; but he certainly has the appearance of one accomplishing a duty or a piece of work which we do not discuss, which is important, necessary and inevitable.

But the lesson suddenly ends with a joke carried rather too far by the pupil, who catches his good master by the seat of his trousers, into which he plants disrespectful teeth. He is severely reprimanded, deprived of his carrots and sent back in disgrace to his private apartments.

13

Next comes Berto, who is like a big, sleek

The Unknown Guest

Norman horse. He makes the calm, digni-
fied, peaceful entrance of a blind giant. His
large, dark, brilliant eyes are quite dead, deprived of any reflex power. He feels about
with his hoof for the board on which he is
to rap his answers. He has not yet gone
beyond the rudiments of mathematics; and
the early part of his education was particularly difficult. They managed to make him
understand the value and meaning of the
numbers and of the addition- and multipli-
cation-signs by means of little taps on his
sides. Krall speaks to him as a father
might speak to the youngest of his sons.
He explains to him fondly the easy sums
which I suggest his doing: two plus three,
eight minus four, four times three; he says:

"Mind! It's not plus three or minus
three this time, but four multiplied by
three!"

Berto hardly ever makes a mistake.
When he does not understand the question,

he waits for it to be written with the finger
on his side; and the careful way in which
he works it out like some backward and
afflicted child is an infinitely pathetic sight.
He is much more zealous and conscientious
than his fellow-pupils; and we feel that, in
the darkness wherein he dwells, this work
is, next to his meals, the only spark of light
and interest in his existence. He will certainly never rival Muhamed, for instance,
who is the arithmetical prodigy, the Inaudi,
of horses; but he is a valuable and living
proof that the theory of unconscious and
imperceptible signs, the only one which the
German theorists have hitherto seriously
considered, is now clearly untenable.

I have not yet spoken of Zarif. He is
not in the best of tempers; and besides, in
arithmetic, he is only a less learned and
more capricious Muhamed. He answers
most of the questions at random, stubbornly
raising his foot and declining to lower it, so

as clearly to mark his disapproval; but he solves the last problem correctly when he is promised a panful of carrots and no more lessons for that morning. The groom enters to lead him away and makes some movement or other at which the horse starts, rears and shies.

"That's his bad conscience," says Krall, gravely.

And the expression assumes a singular meaning and importance in this hybrid atmosphere, steeped in an indefinable something from another world.

But it is half-past one, the sacred German dinner-hour. The horses are taken back to their racks and the men separate, wishing one another the inevitable *Mahlzeit*.

As he walks with me along the quays of the black and muddy Wupper, Krall says:

"It is a pity that you did not see Zarif in one of his better moods. He is sometimes more startling than Muhamed and has given me two or three surprises that seem incredible. One morning, for instance, I came to the stable and was preparing to give him his lesson in arithmetic. He was no sooner in front of the spring-board than he began to stamp with his foot. I left him alone and was astounded to hear a whole sentence, an absolutely human sentence, come letter by letter from his hoof: 'Albert has beaten Hänschen,' was what he said to me that day. Another time, I wrote down from his dictation, 'Hänschen has bitten Kama.' Like a child seeing its father after an absence, he felt the need to inform me of the little doings of the stable; he provided me with the artless chronicle of a humble and uneventful life."

Krall, for that matter, living in the midst of his miracle, seems to think this quite natural and almost inevitable. I, who have been immersed in it for only a few hours,

accept it almost as calmly as he does. I
believe without hesitation what he tells
me; and, in the presence of this phenomenon which, for the first time in man's existence, gives us a sentence that has not
sprung from a human brain, I ask myself
whither we are tending, where we stand and
what lies ahead of us. . . .

14

After dinner, the experiments begin
again, for my host is untiring. First of all,
pointing to me, he asks Muhamed if he remembers what his uncle's name is. The
horse raps out an H. Krall is astonished
and utters fatherly reprimands:

"Come, take care! You know it's not
an H."

The horse raps out an E. Krall becomes
a little impatient: he threatens, he implores,
he promises in turns carrots and the direst
punishments, such as sending for Albert,

the groom, who, on special occasions, recalls idle and inattentive pupils to a sense of duty and decorum, for Krall himself never chastises his horses, lest he should lose their friendship or their confidence. So he continues his reproaches:

"Come now, are you going to be more careful and not rap out your letters anyhow?"

Muhamed obstinately goes his own way and strikes an R. Then Krall's open face lights up:

"He's right," he says. "You understand: H E R, standing for *Herr*. He wanted to give you the title to which every man wearing a top hat or a bowler has the right. He does it only very rarely and I had forgotten all about it. He probably heard me call you Herr Maeterlinck and wanted to get it perfectly. This special politeness and this excess of zeal augur a particularly good lesson. You've done very well, Muhamed, my child; you've done very well and I beg your pardon. Now kiss me and go on."

But Muhamed, after giving his master a hearty kiss, still seems to be hesitating. Then Krall, to put him on the right track, observes that the first letter of my name is the same as the first letter of his own. Muhamed strikes a K, evidently thinking of his master's name. At last, Krall draws a big M on the black-board, whereupon the horse, like one suddenly remembering a word which he could not think of, raps out, one after the other and without stopping, the letters M A Z R L K, which, stripped of useless vowels, represent the curious corruption which my name has undergone, since the morning, in a brain that is not a human brain. He is told that this is not correct. He seems to agree, gropes about a little and writes, M A R Z L E G K. Krall repeats my name and asks which is the first letter to be altered. The stallion marks an R.

"Good, but what letter will you put instead?"

Muhamed strikes an N.

"No, do be careful!"

He strikes a T.

"Very good, but in what place will the T come?"

"In the third," replies the horse; and the corrections continue until my patronymic comes out of its strange adventure almost unscathed.

15

And the spelling, the questioning, the sums, the problems are resumed and follow upon one another, as wonderful, as bewildering as before, but already a little dimmed by familiarity, like any other prolonged miracle. It is important, besides, to notice that the instances which I have given are not to be classed among the most remarkable feats of our magic horses. To-day's is a good ordinary lesson, a respectable lesson, not illumined by flashes of genius. But in the presence of other witnesses the horses performed more startling exploits which broke down even more decisively the barrier, which is undoubtedly an imaginary one, between animal and human nature. One day, for instance, Zarif, the scamp of the party, suddenly stopped in the middle of his lesson. They asked him the reason.

"Because I am tired."

Another time, he answered:

"Pain in my leg."

They recognize and identify pictures shown to them, distinguish colours and scents. I have made a point of stating only what I saw with my own eyes and heard with my own ears; and I declare that I have done so with the same scrupulous accuracy as though I were reporting a criminal trial in which a man's life depended on my evidence.

But I was practically convinced of the truth of the incidents before going to Elberfeld; and it was not to check them that I made the journey. I was anxious to make certain if the telepathic theory, which was the only one that I considered admissible, would withstand the tests which I intended to apply to it. I opened my mind on the subject to Krall, who at first did not quite grasp what I was asking. Like most men who have not made a special study of these questions, he imagined that telepathy meant above all a deliberate and conscious transmission of thought; and he assured me that he never made any effort to transmit his and that, for the most part, the horses gave a reply which was the exact opposite of what he was expecting. I did not doubt this for a moment; in fact, direct and deliberate transmission of thought is, even among men, a very rare, difficult and uncertain phenomenon, whereas involuntary, unpremeditated and unsuspected communications between one subconsciousness and another can no longer be denied except by those who of set purpose ignore studies and experiments that are within the reach of any one who will take the trouble to engage in them. I was persuaded therefore that the horses acted exactly like the "tipping-tables" which simply translate the subliminal ideas of one or other of those present by the aid of conventional little taps. When all is said, it is much less surprising to see a horse than a table lift its foot and much more natural that the living substance of an animal rather than the inert matter of a thing should be sensitive and susceptible to the mysterious influence of a medium. I knew quite well that experiments had been made in order to eliminate this theory. People, for instance, prepared a certain number of questions and placed them in sealed envelopes. Then, on entering the presence of the horse, they would take one of the envelopes at random, open it and write down the problem on the black-board; and Muhamed or Zarif would answer with the same facility and the same readiness as though the solution had been known to all the onlookers. But was it really unknown to their subconsciousness? Who could say for certain? Tests of this kind require extraordinary precautions and a special dexterity; for the action of the subconsciousness is so subtle, takes such unexpected turns, delves in the museum of so many forgotten treasures and operates at such distances that one is never sure of escaping it. Were those precautions taken? I was not convinced that they were; and, without pretending to decide the question, I said to myself that my blissful ignorance of mathematics might perhaps be of service in shedding light upon some part of it.

For this ignorance, however deplorable from other points of view, gave me a rare advantage in this case. It was in fact extremely unlikely that my subliminal consciousness, which had never known what a cubic root was or the root of any other power, could help the horse. I therefore took from a table a list containing several problems, all different and all equally unpleasant-looking, covered up the solutions, asked Krall to leave the stable and, when alone with Zarif, copied out one of them on the black-board. In order not to overload these pages with details which would only be a repetition of one another, I will at once say that none of the antitelepathic tests succeeded that day. It was the end of the lesson and late in the afternoon; the horses were tired and irritable; and, whether Krall was there or not, whether the problem was elementary or difficult, they gave only absurd replies, wilfully "putting their foot in it," as one might say with very good reason. But, next morning, on resuming their task, when I proceeded as described above, Muhamed and Zarif, doubtless in a better temper and already more accustomed to their new examiner, gave in rapid succession correct answers to nearly every problem set them. I am bound in fairness to say that there was no appreciable difference between these results and those which are obtained in the presence of Krall or other onlookers who, consciously or unconsciously, are already aware of the answer required.

I next thought of another and much simpler test, but one which, by virtue of its very simplicity, could not be exposed to any elaborate and far-fetched suspicions. I saw on one of the shelves in the stable a parcel of cards, about the size of an octavo volume, each bearing an arabic numeral on one of its sides. I once more asked my good friend Krall, whose courtesy is inexhaustible, to leave me alone with his pupil. I then shuffled the cards and put three of them in a row on the spring-board in front of the horse, without looking at them myself. There was therefore, at that moment, not a human soul on earth who knew the figures spread at the feet of my companion, this creature so full of mystery that already I no longer dare call him an animal. Without hesitation and unasked, he rapped out correctly the number formed by the cards. The experiment succeeded, as often as I cared to try it, with Hänschen, Muhamed and Zarif alike. Muhamed did even more: as each figure was of a different colour, I asked him to tell me the colour—of which I myself was absolutely ignorant—of the first letter on the right. With the aid of the conventional alphabet, he replied that it was blue, which proved to be the case. Of course, I ought to have multiplied these experiments and made them more exhaustive and complicated by combining, with the aid of the cards and under the same conditions, exercises in multiplication, division and the extracting of roots. I had not the time; but, a few days after I left, the subject was resumed and completed by Dr. H. Hamel. I will sum up his report of the experiments: the doctor, alone in the stable with the horse (Krall was away, travelling), puts down on the black-board the sign $+$ and then places before and after this sign, without looking at either of them, a card marked with a figure which he does not know. He next asks Muhamed to add up the two numbers. Muhamed at first gives a few heedless taps with his hoof. He is called to order and requested to be serious and to attend. He then gives fifteen distinct taps. The doctor next replaces the

sign $+$ by $\times$ and, again without looking
at them, places two cards on the black-
board and asks the horse not to add up the
two figures this time, but to multiply them.
Muhamed taps out, "27," which is right,
for the black-board says, "9 $\times$ 3." The
same success follows with other multiplication-sums: 9 $\times$ 2, 8 $\times$ 6. Then the doctor
takes from an envelope a problem of which
he does not know the solution: $\sqrt[4]{7890481}$.
Muhamed replies, "53." The doctor looks
at the back of the paper: once more, the
answer is perfectly correct.

16

Does this mean that every risk of
telepathy is done away with? It would
perhaps be rash to make a categorical assertion. The power and extent of telepathy
are as yet, we cannot too often repeat, indefinite, indiscernible, untraceable and un-
limited. We have but quite lately discov-

ered it, we know only that its existence can no longer be denied; but, as for all the rest, we are at much the same stage as that whereat Galvani was when he gave life to the muscles of his dead frogs with two little plates of metal which roused the jeers of the scientists of his time, but contained the germ of all the wonders of electricity.

Nevertheless, as regards telepathy in the sense in which we understand and know it to-day, my mind is made up. I am persuaded that it is not in this direction that we must seek for an explanation of the phenomenon; or, if we are determined to find it there, the explanation becomes complicated with so many subsidiary mysteries that it is better to accept the prodigy as it stands, in its original obscurity and simplicity. When, for instance, I was copying out one of the grisly problems which I have mentioned, it is quite certain that my conscious intelligence could make neither head nor tail of it. I did not so much as know what it meant or whether the exponent 3 . 4 . 5 called for a multiplication, a division or some other mathematical operation which I did not even try to imagine; and, rack my memory as I may, I cannot remember any moment in my life when I knew more about it than I do now. We should therefore have to admit that my subliminal self is a born mathematician, quick, infallible and endowed with boundless learning. It is possible and I fell a certain pride at the thought. But the theory simply shifts the miracle by making it pass from the horse's soul to mine; and the miracle becomes no clearer by the transfer, which, for that matter, does not sound probable. I need hardly add that, *a fortiori*, Dr. Hamel's experiments and many others which I have not here the space to describe finally dispose of the theory.

Let us see how those who have interested themselves in these extraordinary
manifestations have attempted to explain
them.

As we go along, we will just shear
through the feeble undergrowth of childish
theories. I shall not, therefore, linger over
the suggestions of cheating, of manifest
signs addressed to the eye or ear, of elec-
trical installations that are supposed to
control the answers, nor other idle tales of
an excessively clumsy character. To realize
their inexcusable inanity we have but to
spend a few minutes in the honest Elberfeld stable.

At the beginning of this essay, I mentioned the attack made by Herr Pfungst.
Herr Pfungst, the reader will remember,
claims to prove that all the horse's replies
are determined by imperceptible and probably unconscious movement on the part of

the person putting the questions. This interpretation, which falls to the ground, like all the others, in the face of the actual facts, would not deserve serious discussion, were it not that the Berlin psychologist's report created an immense sensation some years ago and has succeeded in intimidating the greater part of the official German scientific world to this day. It is true that the report in question is a monument of useless pedantry, but we are none the less bound to admit that, such as it was, it annihilated poor Von Osten, who, being no controversialist and not knowing how to proclaim the truth which was struggling for utterance, died in gloom and solitude.

To make an end of this cumbrous and puerile theory, is it necessary to emphasize again that experiments in which the animal does not see the questioner are as regularly successful as the others? Krall, if you ask him, will stand behind the horse, will speak from the end of the room, will leave the stable altogether; and the results are just the same. They are the same again when the tests are made in the dark or when the animal's head is covered with a close-fitting hood. They do not vary either in the case of Berto, who is stone-blind, or when any other person whatever sets the problem in Krall's absence. Will it be maintained that this outsider or that stranger is acquainted beforehand with the imperceptible signs that are to dictate the solution which he himself often does not know?

But what is the use of prolonging this fight against a cloud of smoke? None of it can bear examination; and it calls for a genuine effort of the will to set one's self seriously to refute such pitiful objections.

18

On the ground thus cleared and at the

portal of this unlooked-for riddle, which comes to disturb our peace in a region which we thought to be finally explored and conquered, there are only two ways, if not of explaining, at least of contemplating the phenomenon: to admit purely and simply the almost human intelligence of the horse, or to have recourse to an as yet very vague and indefinite theory which, for lack of a better designation, we will call the mediumistic or subliminal theory and of which we will strive presently—and no doubt vainly —to dispel the grosser darkness. But, whatever interpretation we adopt, we are bound to recognize that it plunges us into a mystery which is equally profound and equally astonishing on either side, one directly related to the greatest mysteries that overwhelm us; and it is open to us to accept it with resignation or rejoicing, according as we prefer to live in a world wherein everything is within the reach of our intelligence or a world wherein everything is incomprehensible.

As for Krall, he does not doubt for an instant that his horses solve for themselves, without any assistance, without any outside influence, simply by their own mental powers, the most arduous problems set them. He is persuaded that they understand what is said to them and what they say, in short, that their brain and their will perform exactly the same functions as a human brain and will. It is certain that the facts seem to prove him right and that his opinion carries very great weight, for, after all, he knows his horses better than any one does; he has beheld the birth or rather the awakening of that dormant intelligence, even as a mother beholds the birth or the awakening of intelligence in her child; he has perceived its first gropings, known its first resistance and its first triumphs; he has watched it taking shape, breaking away and gradually rising to the point at which it stands to-day; in a word, he is the father and the principal and sole perpetual witness of the miracle.

19

Yes, but the miracle comes as such a surprise that, the moment we set foot in it, a sort of instinctive aberration seizes us, refusing to accept the evidence and compelling us to search in every direction to see if there is not another outlet. Even in the presence of those astounding horses and while they are working before our eyes, we do not yet sincerely believe that which fills and subdues our gaze. We accept the facts, because there is no means of escaping them; but we accept them only provisionally and with all reserve, putting off till later the comfortable explanation which will give us back our familiar, shallow certainties. But the explanation does not come; there is none in the homely and not very lofty regions wherein we hoped to find one; there is neither fault nor flaw in the mighty evidence; and nothing delivers us from the mystery.

It must be confessed that this mystery, springing from a point where we least expected to come upon the unknown, bears enough within itself to scatter all our convictions. Remember that, since man appeared upon this earth, he has lived among creatures which, from immemorial experience, he thought that he knew as perfectly as he knows an object fashioned by his hands. Out of these creatures he chose the most docile and, as he called them, the most intelligent, attaching in this case to the word intelligence a sense so narrow as to be almost ridiculous. He observed them, scrutinized them, tried them, analyzed them and dissected them in every imaginable way; and whole lives were devoted to nothing but the study of their habits, their faculties, their nervous system, their pathology, their psychology, their instincts. All this led to certainties which, among those supported by our unexplained little existence on an inexplicable planet, would seem to be the least doubtful, the least subject to revision. There is no disputing, for instance, that the horse is gifted with an extraordinary memory, that he possesses the sense of direction, that he understands a few signs and even a few words and that he obeys them. It is equally undeniable that the anthropoid apes are capable of imitating a great number of our actions and of our attitudes; but it is also manifest that their bewildered and feverish imagination perceives neither their object nor their scope. As for the dog, the one of all these privileged animals who lives closest to us, who for thousands and thousands of years has eaten at our table and worked with us

288

and been our friend, it is manifest that, now and then, we catch a rather uncanny gleam in his deep, watchful eyes. It is certain that he sometimes wanders in a curious fashion along the mysterious border that separates our own intelligence from that which we grant to the other creatures inhabiting this earth with us. But it is no less certain that he has never definitely passed it. We know exactly how far he can go; and we have invariably found that our efforts, our patience, our encouragement, our passionate appeals have hitherto failed to draw him out of the somewhat narrow, darkly enchanted circle wherein nature seems to have imprisoned him once and for all.

20

There remains, it is true, the insect-world, in which marvellous things happen. It includes architects, geometricians, mechanicians, engineers, weavers, physicists, chemists and surgeons who have forestalled most of our human inventions. I need not here remind the reader of the wasps' and bees' genius for building, the social and economic organization of the hive and the ant-hill, the spider's snares, the eumenes' nest and hanging egg, the odynerus' cell with its neat stacks of game, the sacred beetle's filthy but ingenius ball, the leaf-cutter's faultless disks, the brick-laying of the mason-bee, the three dagger-thrusts which the sphex administers to the three nerve-centres of the cricket, the lancet of the cerceris, who paralyses her victims without killing them and preserves them for an indefinite period as fresh meat, nor a thousand other features which it would be impossible to enumerate without recapitulating the whole of Henri Fabre's work and completely altering the proportions of the present essay. But here such silence and such darkness reign that we have nothing to hope for. There exists, so to speak, no bench-mark, no means of communication between the world of insects and our own; and we are perhaps less far from grasping and fathoming what takes place in Saturn or Jupiter than what is enacted in the anthill or the hive. We know absolutely nothing of the quality, the number, the extent or even the nature of their senses. Many of the great laws on which our life is based do not exist for them: those, for instance, which govern fluids are completely reversed. They seem to inhabit our planet, but in reality move in an entirely different world. Understanding nothing of their intelligence pierced with disconcerting gaps, in which the blindest stupidity suddenly comes and destroys the ablest and most inspired schemes, we have given the name of instinct to that which we could not apprehend, postponing our interpretation of a word that touches upon life's most insoluble riddles. There is, therefore, from the point of view of the intellectual faculties, nothing to be gathered from those extraordinary creatures who are not, like the other animals, our "lesser brothers," but strangers, aliens from we know not where, survivors or percursors of another world.

2 1

We were at this stage, slumbering peacefully in our long-established convictions, when a man entered upon the scene and suddenly showed us that we were wrong and that, for long centuries, we had overlooked a truth which was scarcely even covered with a very thin veil. And the strangest thing is that this astonishing discovery is in no wise the natural consequence of a new invention, of processes or methods hitherto unknown. It owes nothing to the latest acquirements of our knowledge. It springs from the humblest idea which the most primitive man might have conceived in the first days of the earth's existence. It is simply a matter of having a little more patience, confidence and respect for all that which shares our lot in a world whereof we know none of the purposes. It is simply a matter of having a little less pride and of looking a little more fraternally upon existences that are much more fraternal than we believed. There is no secret about the almost puerile ingenuousness of Von Osten's methods and Krall's. They start with the principle that the horse is an ignorant but intelligent child; and they treat him as such. They speak, explain, demonstrate, argue and mete out rewards or punishments like a schoolmaster addressing little boys of five or six. They begin by placing a few skittle-pins in front of their strange pupil. They count them and make him count them by alternately lifting and lowering the horse's hoof. He thus obtains his first notion of numbers. They next add one or two more skittles and say, for instance:

"Three skittles and two skittles are five skittles."

In this way, they explain and teach addition; next, by the reverse process, subtraction, which is followed by multiplication, division and all the rest.

At the beginning, the lessons are extremely laborious and demand an untiring and loving patience, which is the whole secret of the miracle. But, as soon as the first barrier of darkness is passed, the progress becomes bewilderingly rapid.

All this is incontestable; and the facts are there, before which we must needs bow. But what upsets all our convictions or, more correctly, all the prejudices which thousands of years have made as invincible as axioms, what we do not succeed in understanding is that the horse at once understands what we

want of him; it is that first step, the first
tremor of an unexpected intelligence, which
suddenly reveals itself as human. At what
precise second did the light appear and was
the veil rent asunder? It is impossible to
say; but it is certain that, at a given moment, without any visible sign to reveal the
prodigious inner transformation, the horse
acts and replies as though he suddenly understood the speech of man. What is it
that sets the miracle working? We know
that, after a time, the horse associates certain words with certain objects that interest
him or with three or four events whose infinite repetition forms the humble tissue of
his daily life. This is only a sort of mechanical memory which has nothing in common with the most elementary intelligence.
But behold, one fine day, without any per-
ceptible transition, he seems to know the
meaning of a host of words which possess
no interest for him; which represent to him

no picture, no memory; which he has never had occasion to connect with any sensation, agreeable or disagreeable. He handles figures which even to man are nothing but obscure and abstract ideas. He solves problems that cannot possibly be made objective or concrete. He reproduces letters which, from his point of view, correspond with nothing actual. He fixes his attention and makes observations on things or circumstances which in no way affect him, which remain and always will remain alien and indifferent to him. In a word, he steps out of the narrow ring in which he was made to turn by hunger and fear—which have been described as the two great moving powers of all that is not human—to enter the immense circle in which sensations go on being shed till ideas come into view.

22

Is it possible to believe that the horses

really do what they appear to do? Is there
no precedent for the marvel? Is there no
transition between the Elberfeld stallions
and the horses which we have known until
this day? It is not easy to answer these
questions, for it is only since yesterday that
the intellectual powers of our defenceless
brothers have been subjected to strictly
scientific experiments. We have, it is true,
more than one collection of anecdotes in
which the intelligence of animals is lauded
to the skies; but we cannot rely upon these
ill-authenticated stories. To find genuine
and incontestable instances we must have
recourse to the works, rare as yet, of scientific men who have made a special study of
the subject. M. Hachet-Souplet, for example, the director of the Institut de Psy-
chologie Zoologique, mentions the case of
a dog who learnt to acquire an abstract
idea of weight. You put in front of him
eight rounded and polished stones, all of

exactly the same size and shape, but of different weights. You tell him to fetch the heaviest or the lightest; he judges their weight by lifting them and, without mistake, picks out the one required.

The same writer also tells the story of a parrot to whom he had taught the word "cupboard" by showing him a little box that could be hung up on the wall at different heights and in which his daily allowance of food was always ostentatiously put away:

"I next taught him the names of a number of objects," says M. Hachet-Souplet, "by holding them out to him. Among them was a ladder; and I prevailed upon the bird to say, 'Climb,' each time that he saw me mount the steps. One morning, when the parrot's cage was brought into the laboratory, the cupboard was hanging near the ceiling, while the little ladder was stowed away in a corner among other objects familiar to the bird. Now the parrot, every day, when I opened the cupboard, used to scream, 'Cupboard! Cupboard! Cupboard!' with all his might. My problem was, therefore, this: seeing that the cupboard was out of my reach and that, therefore, I could not take his food out of it; knowing, on the other hand, that I was able to raise myself above the level of the floor by climbing the ladder; and having the words 'climb' and 'ladder' at his disposal: would he employ them to suggest to me the idea of using them in order to reach the cupboard? Greatly excited, the parrot flapped his wings, bit the bars of his cage, and screamed:

" 'Cupboard! Cupboard! Cupboard!'

"And I got no more out of him that day. The next day, the bird, having received nothing but millet, for which he did not much care, instead of the hemp-seed con-

tained in the cupboard, was in paroxysms
of anger; and, after he had made numberless attempts to force open his bars, his
attention was at last caught by the ladder
and he said:

" 'Ladder, climb, cupboard!' "

We have here, as the author remarks, a
marvellous intellectual effort. There is an
evident association of ideas; cause is linked
with effect; and examples such as this les-
sen appreciably the distance separating our
learned horses from their less celebrated
brethren. We must admit, however, that
this intellectual effort, if we observe animals
a little carefully, is much less uncommon
than we think. It surprises us in this case
because a special and, when all is said,
purely mechanical arrangement of the parrot's organ gives him a human voice. At
every moment, I find in my own dog associations of ideas no less evident and often

more complex. For instance, if he is thirsty, he seeks my eyes and next looks at the tap in the dressing-room, thus showing that he very plainly connects the notions of thirst, running water and human intervention. When I dress to go out, he evidently watches all my movements. While I am lacing my boots, he conscientiously licks my hands, in order that my divinity may be good to him and especially to congratulate me on my capital idea of going out for a constitutional. It is a sort of general and as yet vague approval. Boots promise an excursion out of doors, that is to say, space, fragrant roads, long grass full of surprises, corners scented with offal, friendly or tragic encounters and the pursuit of wholly illusory game. But the fair vision is still in anxious suspense. He does not yet know if he is going with me. His fate is now being decided; and his eyes, melting with anguish, devour my mind. If I buckle on my leather gaiters, it means the sudden and utter extinction of all that constitutes the joy of life. They leave not a ray of hope. They herald the hateful, lonely motor-cycle, which he cannot keep up with; and he stretches himself sadly in a dark corner, where he goes back to the gloomy dreams of an unoccupied, forsaken dog. But, when I slip my arms into the sleeves of my heavy great-coat, one would think that they were opening the gates of the most dazzling paradise. For this implies the car, the obvious, indubitable motor-car, in other words, the radiant summit of the most superlative delight. And delirious barks, inordinate bounds, riotous, embarrassing demonstrations of affection greet a happiness which, for all that, is but an immaterial idea, built up of artless memories and ingenuous hopes.

23

I mention these matters only because they

are quite ordinary and because there is nobody who has not made a thousand similar
observations. As a rule, we do not notice
that these humble manifestations represent
sentiments, associations of ideas, inferences,
deductions, an absolute and altogether human mental effort. They lack only speech;
but speech is merely a mechanical accident
which reveals the operations of thought
more clearly to us. We are amazed that
Muhamed or Zarif should recognize the
picture of a horse, a donkey, a hat, or a
man on horseback, or that they should spontaneously report to their master the little
events that happen in the stable; but it is
certain that our own dog is incessantly per-
forming a similar work and that his eyes,
if we could read them, would tell us a great
deal more. The primary miracle of Elberfeld is that the stallions should have been
given the means of expressing what they
think and feel. It is momentous; but, when

closely looked into, it is not incomprehensible. Between the talking horses and my silent dog there is an enormous distance, but not an abyss. I am saying this not to detract from the nature or extent of the prodigy, but to call attention to the fact that the theory of animal intelligence is more justifiable and less fanciful than one is at first inclined to think.

24

But the second and greater miracle is that man should have been able to rouse the horse from his immemorial sleep, to fix and direct his attention and to interest him in matters that are more foreign and indifferent to him than the variations of temperature in Sirius or Aldebaran are to us. It really seems, when we consider our preconceived ideas, that there is not in the animal an organic and insurmountable inability to do what man's brain does, a total and irremediable absence of intellectual faculties, but rather a profound lethargy and torpor of those faculties. It lives in a sort of undisturbed stolidity, of nebulous slumber. As Dr. Ochorowicz very justly remarks, "its waking state is very near akin to the state of a man walking in his sleep." Having no notion of space or time, it spends its life, one may say, in a perpetual dream. It does what is strictly necessary to keep itself alive; and all the rest passes over it and does not penetrate at all into its hermetically closed imaginings. Exceptional circumstances—some extraordinary need, wish, passion or shock—are required to produce what M. Hachet-Souplet calls "the psychic flash" which suddenly thaws and galvanizes its brain, placing it for a minute in the waking state in which the human brain works normally. Nor is this surprising. It does not need that awakening in order to exist; and we know that nature never makes great superfluous efforts.

"The intellect," as Professor Clarapède well says, "appears only as a makeshift, an instrument which betrays that the organism is not adapted to its environment, a mode of expression which reveals a state of impotence."

It is probable that our brain at first suffered from the same lethargy, a condition, for that matter, from which many men have not yet emerged; and it is even more probable that, compared with other modes of existence, with other psychic phenomena, on another plane and in another sphere, the dense sleep in which we move is similar to that in which the lower animals have their being. It also is traversed, with increasing frequency, by psychic flashes of a different order and a different scope. Seeing, on the one side, the intellectual movement that seems to be spreading among our lesser brothers and, on the other, the ever more constantly repeated manifestations of our subconsciousness, we might even ask ourselves if we have not here, on two different planes, a tension, a parallel pressure, a new desire, a new attempt of the mysterious spiritual force which animates the universe and which seems to be incessantly seeking fresh outlets and fresh conducting-rods. Be this as it may, when the flash has passed, we behave very much as the animals do: we promptly lapse into the indifferent sleep which suffices also for our miserable ways. We ask no more of it, we do not follow the luminous trail that summons us to an unknown world, we go on turning in our dismal circle, like contented sleep-walkers, while Isis' sistrum rattles without respite to rouse the faithful.

25

I repeat, the great miracle of Elberfeld is that of having been able to prolong and reproduce at will those isolated "psychic flashes." The horses, in comparison with the other animals, are here in the state of a man whose subliminal consciousness had gained the upper hand. That man would lead a higher existence, in an almost immaterial atmosphere, of which the phenomena of metaphysics, sparks falling from a region which we shall perhaps one day reach, sometimes give us an uncertain and fleeting glimpse. Our intelligence, which is really lethargy and which keeps us imprisoned in a little hollow of space and time, would there be replaced by intuition, or rather by a sort of immanent knowledge which would forthwith make us sharers in all that is known to a universe which perhaps knows all things. Unfortunately, we have not, or at least, unlike the horses, we are not acquainted with a superior being who interests himself in us and helps us to throw off our torpor. We have to become our own god, to rise above ourselves and to keep ourselves raised by our unaided strength. It is almost certain that the horse would never have come out of his nebulous sphere without man's assistance; but it is not forbidden to hope that man, with no other help than his own courage and high purpose, may yet succeed in breaking through the sleep that cramps him and blinds him.

26

To come back then to our horses and to the main point, which is the isolated "psychic flash," it is admitted that they know the values of figures, that they can distinguish and identify smells, colours, forms, objects and even graphic reproductions of those objects. They also understand a large number of words, including some of which they were never taught the meaning, but which they picked up as they went along by hearing them spoken around them. They have learnt, with the assistance of an exceedingly complicated alphabet, to reproduce the words, thanks to which they manage to convey impressions, sensations, wishes, associations of ideas, observations and even spontaneous reflections. It has been held that all this implies real acts of intelligence. It is, in fact, often very difficult to decide exactly how far it is intelligence and how far memory, instinct, imitative genius, obedience or mechanical impulse, the effects of training, or happy coincidences.

There are cases, however, which admit of little or no hesitation. I give a few.

One day Krall and his collaborator, Dr. Schöller, thought that they would try and teach Muhamed to express himself in speech. The horse, a docile and eager pupil, made touching and fruitless efforts to reproduce human sounds. Suddenly, he stopped and, in his strange phonetic spelling, declared, by striking his foot on the spring-board:

"*Ig hb kein gud Sdim:* I have not a good voice."

Observing that he did not open his mouth, they strove to make him understand, by the example of a dog, with pictures, and so on, that, in order to speak, it is necessary to separate the jaws. They next asked him:

"What must you do to speak?"

He replied, by striking with his foot:

"Open mouth."

"Why don't you open yours?"

"*Weil kan nigd:* because I can't."

A few days after, Zarif was asked how he talks to Muhamed.

"*Mit Munt:* with mouth."

"Why don't you tell me that with your mouth?"

"*Weil ig kein Stim hbe:* because I have no voice."

Does not this answer, as Krall remarks,
allow us to suppose that he has other means
than speech of conversing with his stable-
companion?

In the course of another lesson, Muhamed was shown the portrait of a young
girl whom he did not know.

"What's that?" asked his master.

"Metgen: a girl?"

On the black-board:

"Why is it a girl?"

"Weil lang Hr hd: because she has long
hair."

"And what has she not?"

"Moustache."

They next produced the likeness of a
man with no moustache.

"What's this?"

"Man."

"Why is it a man?"

"Weil kurz Hr had: because he has
short hair."

The Unknown Guest

I could multiply these examples indefinitely by drawing on the voluminous Elberfeld minutes, which, I may say in passing, have the convincing force of photographic records. All this, it must be agreed, is unexpected and disconcerting, had never been foreseen or suspected and may be regarded as one of the strangest prodigies, one of the most stupefying revelations that have taken place since man has dwelt in this world of riddles. Nevertheless, by reflecting, by comparing, by investigating, by regarding certain forgotten or neglected landmarks and starting-points, by taking into consideration the thousand imperceptible gradations between the greatest and the least, the highest and the lowest, it is still possible to explain, admit and understand. We can, if it comes to that, imagine that, in his secret self, in his tragic silence, our dog also makes similar remarks and reflections. Once again, the miraculous bridge

which, in this instance, spans the gulf between the animal and man is much more
the expression of thought than thought itself. We may go further and grant that
certain elementary calculations, such as
little additions, little subtractions of one or
two figures, are, after all, conceivable; and
I, for my part, am inclined to believe that
the horse really executes them. But where
we get out of our depth, where we enter
into the realm of pure enchantment is when
it becomes a matter of mathematical operations on a large scale, notably of the finding
of roots. We know, for instance, that the
extraction of the fourth root of a number
of six figures calls for eighteen multiplications, ten subtractions and three divisions
and that the horse does thirty-one sums in
five or six seconds, that is to say,
during the brief, careless glance which
he gives at the black-board on which
the problem is inscribed, as though the

answer came to him intuitively and instantaneously.

Still, if we admit the theory of intelligence, we must also admit that the horse knows what he is doing, since it is not until after learning what a squared number or a square root means that he appears to understand or that, at any rate, he gradually works out correctly the ever more complicated calculations required of him. It is not possible to give here the details of this instruction, which was astonishingly rapid. The reader will find them on pages 117 *et seq.* of Krall's book, *Denkende Tiere.* Krall begins by explaining to Muhamed that 2^2 is equal to $2 \times 2 = 4$; that 2^3 is equal to $2 \times 2 \times 2 = 6$; that 2 is the square root of 4; and so on. In short, the explanations and demonstrations are absolutely similar to those which one would give to an extremely intelligent child, with this difference, that the horse is much more attentive than the child and that, thanks to his extraordinary memory, he never forgets what he appears to have understood. Let us add, to complete the magical and incredible character of the phenomenon that, according to Krall's own statement, the horse was not taught beyond the point of extracting the square root of the number 144 and that he spontaneously invented the manner of extracting all the others.

27

Must we once more repeat, in connection with these startling performances, that those who speak of audible or visible signals, of telegraphy and wireless telegraphy, of expedients, trickery or deceit, are speaking of what they do not know and of what they have not seen? There is but one reply to be made to any one who honestly refuses to believe:

"Go to Elberfeld—the problem is suffi-

ciently important, sufficiently big with consequences to make the journey worth while
—and, behind closed doors, alone with the
horse, in the absolute solitude and silence of
the stable, set Muhamed to extract half-a-
dozen roots which, like that which I have
mentioned, require thirty-one operations.
You must yourself be ignorant of the solutions, so as to do away with any transmission of unconscious thought. If he then
gives you, one after the other, five or six
correct solutions, as he did to me and many
others, you will not go away with the conviction that the animal is able by its intelligence to extract those roots, because
that conviction would upset too thoroughly
the greater part of the certainties on which
your life is based; but you will, at any rate,
be persuaded that you have been for a few
minutes in the presence of one of the greatest and strangest riddles that can disturb
the mind of man; and it is always a good

and salutary thing to come into contact with emotions of this order."

28

Truth to say, the theory of intelligence in the animal would be so extraordinary as to be almost untenable. If we are determined, at whatever cost, to pin our faith to it, we are bound to call in the aid of other ideas, to appeal, for instance, to the extremely mysterious and essentially uncomprehended and incomprehensible nature of numbers. It is almost certain that the science of mathematics lies outside the intelligence. It forms a mechanical and abstract whole, more spiritual than material and more material than spiritual, visible only through its shadow and yet constituting the most immovable of the realities that govern the universe. From first to last it declares itself a very strange force and, as it were, the sovereign of another element than that which nourishes our brain. Secret, indifferent, imperious and implacable, it subjugates and oppresses us from a great height or a great depth, in any case, from very far, without telling us why. One might say that figures place those who handle them in a special condition. They draw the cabalistic circle around their victim. Henceforth, he is no longer his own master, he renounces his liberty, he is literally "possessed" by the powers which he invokes. He is dragged he knows not whither, into a formless, boundless immensity, subject to laws that have nothing human about them, in which each of those lively and tyrannical little signs which move and dance in their thousands under the pen represents nameless, but eternal, invincible and inevitable verities. We think that we are directing them and they enslave us. We become weary and breathless following them into their uninhabitable spaces.

When we touch them, we let loose a force which we are no longer able to control. They do with us what they will and always end by hurling us, blinded and benumbed, into blank infinity or upon a wall of ice against which every effort of our mind and will is shattered.

It is possible, therefore, in the last resort, to explain the Elberfeld mystery by the no less obscure mystery that surrounds numbers. This really only means moving to another spot in the gloom; but it is often just by that moving to another spot that we end by discovering the little gleam of light which shows us a thoroughfare. In any case, and to return to more precise ideas, more than one instance has been cited to prove that the gift of handling great groups of figures is almost independent of the intelligence proper. One of the most curious is that of an Italian shepherd-boy, Vito Mangiamele, who was brought

before the Paris Academy of Science in
1837 and who, at the age of ten, though devoid of the most rudimentary education,
was able in half a minute to extract the
cubic root of a number of seven figures.
Another, more striking still, also mentioned
by Dr. Clarapède in his paper on the
learned horses, is that of a man blind from
birth, an inmate of the lunatic-asylum at
Armentières. This blind man, whose name
is Fleury, a degenerate and nearly an idiot,
can calculate in one minute and fifteen seconds the number of seconds in thirty-nine
years, three months and twelve days, not
forgetting the leap-years. They explain to
him what a square root is, without telling
him the conventional method of finding it;
and soon he extracts almost as rapidly as
Inaudi himself, without a blunder, the
square roots of numbers of four figures,
giving the remainder. On the other hand,
we know that a mathematical genius like

Henri Poincaré confessed himself incapable
of adding up a column of figures without
a mistake.

29

From the maybe enchanted atmosphere
that surrounds numbers we shall pass more
easily to the even more magic mists of the
final theory, the only one remaining to us
for the moment: the mediumistic or subliminal theory. This, we must remember,
is not the telepathic theory proper which
decisive experiments have made us reject.
Let us have the courage to venture upon
it. When one can no longer interpret a
phenomenon by the known, we must needs
try to do so by the unknown. We, therefore, now enter a new province of a great
unexplored kingdom, in which we shall find
ourselves without a guide.

Mediumistic phenomena, manifestations
of the secondary or the subliminal consciousness, between man and man, are, as

we have more than once had occasion to assure ourselves, capricious, undisciplined, evasive and uncertain, but more frequent than one thought and, to one who examines them seriously and honestly, often undeniable. Have similar manifestations been discovered between man and the animals? The study of these manifestations, which is very difficult even in the case of man, becomes still more so when we question witnesses doomed to silence. There are, however, some animals which are looked upon as "psychic," which, in other words, seem indisputably to be sensitive to certain subliminal influences. One usually classes the cat, the dog and the horse in this somewhat ill-defined category. To these superstitious animals one might perhaps add certain birds, more or less birds of omen, and even a few insects, notably the bees. Other animals, such as, for instance, the elephant and the monkey, appear to be proof against

mystery. Be this as it may, M. Ernest
Bozzano, in an excellent article on *Les Perceptions psychiques des animaux*,[1] collected
in 1905 sixty-nine cases of telepathy, presentiments and hallucinations of sight or
hearing in which the principal actors are
cats, dogs and horses. There are, even
among them, ghosts or phantoms of dogs
which, after their death, return to haunt
the homes in which they were happy. Most
of these cases are taken from the *Proceedings of the S. P. R.*, that is to say, they
have nearly all been very strictly investigated. It is impossible, short of filling
these pages with often striking and touching but rather cumbersome anecdotes, to
enumerate them here, however briefly. It
will be sufficient to note that sometimes the
dog begins to howl at the exact moment
when his master loses his life, for instance,

[1] *Annales des sciences psychiques,* August, 1905, pp.
422-469.

on a battlefield, hundreds of miles from the place where the dog is. More commonly, the cat, the dog and the horse plainly manifest that they perceive, often before men do, telepathic apparitions, phantasms of the living or the dead. Horses in particular seem very sensitive to places that pass as haunted or uncanny. On the whole, the result of these observations is that we can hardly dispute that these animals communicate as much as we do and perhaps in the same fashion with the mystery that lies around us. There are moments at which, like man, they see the invisible and perceive events, influences and emotions that are beyond the range of their normal senses. It is, therefore, permissible to believe that their nervous system or some remote or secret part of their being contains the same psychic elements connecting them with an unknown that inspires them with as much terror as it does ourselves.

And, let us say in passing, this terror is rather strange; for, after all, what have they to fear from a phantom or an apparition, they who, we are convinced, have no after-life and who ought, therefore, to remain perfectly indifferent to the manifestations of a world in which they will never set foot?

I shall perhaps be told that it is not certain that these apparitions are objective, that they correspond with an external reality, but that it is exceedingly possible that they spring solely from the man's or the animal's brain. This is not the moment to discuss this very obscure point, which raises the whole question of the supernatural and all the problems of the hereafter. The only important thing to observe is that at one time it is man who transmits his terror, his perception or his idea of the invisible to the animal and at another the animal which transmits its sensations to man. We have here, therefore, intercommunications which spring from a deeper common source than any that we know and which, to issue from it or go back to it, pass through other channels than those of our customary senses. Now all this belongs to that unexplained sensibility, to that secret treasure, to that as yet undetermined psychic power which, for lack of a better term, we call subconsciousness or subliminal consciousness. Moreover, it is not surprising that, in the animals, these subliminal faculties not only exist, but are perhaps keener and more active than in ourselves, because it is our conscious and abnormally individualized life that atrophies them by relegating them to a state of idleness wherein they have fewer and fewer opportunities of being exercised, whereas in our brothers who are less detached from the universe, consciousness—if we can give that name to a very uncertain and confused notion of the ego—is reduced to a few elementary actions. They are much less separated than ourselves from the whole of the circumambient life and they still possess a number of those more general and indeterminate senses whereof we have been deprived by the gradual encroachment of a narrow and intolerant special faculty, our intelligence. Among these senses which up to the present we have described as instincts, for want—and it is becoming a pressing want—of a more suitable and definite word, need I mention the sense of direction, migration, foreknowledge of the weather, of earthquakes and avalanches and many others which we doubtless do not even suspect? Does all this not belong to a subconsciousness which differs from ours only in being so much richer?

30

I am fully aware that this explanation by

means of the subliminal consciousness will not explain very much and will at most invoke the aid of the unknown to illuminate the incomprehensible. But to explain a phenomenon, as Dr. J. de Modzelwski very truly says, "is to put forward a theory which is more familiar and more easily comprehensible to us than the phenomenon at issue." This is really what we are constantly and almost exclusively doing in physics, chemistry, biology and in every branch of science without exception. To explain a phenomenon is not necessarily to make it as clear and pellucid as that two and two are four; and, even so, the fact that two and two are four is not, when we go to the bottom of things, as clear and pellucid as it seems. What in this case, as in most others, we wrongfully call explaining is simply confronting the unexpected mystery which these horses offer us with a few phenomena which are themselves unknown, but which have been perceived longer and more frequently. And this same mystery, thus explained, will serve one day to explain others. It is in this way that science goes to work. We must not blame it: it does what it can; and it does not appear that there are other ways.

31

If we assent to this explanation by means of the subliminal consciousness, which is a sort of mysterious participation in all that happens in this world and the others, many obstacles disappear and we enter into a new region in which we draw strangely nearer to the animals and really become their brothers by closer links, perhaps the only essential links in life. They take part from that moment in the great human problems, in the extraordinary actions of our unknown guest; and, if, since we have been observing the indwelling force more attentively, nothing any longer surprises us of that which it realizes in us, no more should anything surprise us of that which it realizes in them. We are on the same plane with them, in some as yet undetermined element, where it is no longer the intelligence that reigns alone, but another spiritual power, which pays no heed to the brain, which passes by other roads and which might rather be the psychic substance of the universe itself, no longer set in grooves, isolated and specialized by man, but diffused, multiform and perhaps, if we could trace it, equal in everything that exists.

There is, henceforth, no reason why the horses should not participate in most of the mediumistic phenomena which we find existing between man and man; and their mystery ceases to be distinct from those of human metaphysics. If their subliminal is akin to ours, we can begin by extending to its utmost limits the telepathic theory, which has, so to speak, no limits, for, in the matter of telepathy, as Myers has said, all that we are permitted to declare is that "life has the power of manifesting itself to life." We may ask ourselves, therefore, if the problem which I set to the horse, without knowing the terms of it, is not communicated to my subliminal, which is ignorant of it, by that of the horse, who has read it. It is practically certain that this is possible between human subliminals. Is it I who see the solution and transmit it to the horse, who only repeats it to me? But, suppose that it is a problem which I myself am incapable of solving? Whence does the solution come, then? I do not know if the experiment has been attempted, under the same conditions, with a human medium. For that matter, if it succeeded, it would be very much the same as the no less subliminal phenomenon of the arithmetical prodigies, or lightning calculators, with which, in this rather superhuman atmosphere, we are almost forced to compare the riddle of the mathematical horses. Of all the interpretations, it is the one which, for the moment, appears to me the least eccentric and the most natural.

We have seen that the gift of handling colossal figures is almost foreign to the intelligence proper; one can even declare that, in certain cases, it is evidently and completely independent of such intelligence. In these cases, the gift is manifested prior to any education and from the earliest years of childhood. If we refer to the list of arithmetical prodigies given by Dr. Scripture,[1] we see that the faculty made its appearance in Ampère at the age of three, in Colburn at six, in Gauss at three, in Mangiamele at ten, in Safford at six, in Whateley at three, and so on. Generally, it lasts for only a few years, becoming

[1] *American Journal of Psychology,* 1 April 1891.

rapidly enfeebled with age and usually vanishing suddenly at the moment when its possessor begins to go to school.

When you ask those children and even most of the lightning calculators who have come to man's estate how they go to work to solve the huge and complicated problems set them, they reply that they know nothing about it. Bidder, for instance, declares that it is impossible for him to say how he can instinctively tell the logarithm of a number consisting of seven or eight figures. It is the same with Safford, who, at the age of ten, used to do in his head, without ever making a mistake, multiplication-sums the result of which ran into thirty-six figures. The solution presents itself authoritatively and spontaneously; it is a vision, an impression, an inspiration, an intuition coming one knows not whence, suddenly and indubitably. As a rule, they do not even try to calculate. Contrary to the general belief, they have no peculiar methods; or, if method there be, it is more a practical way of subdividing the intuition. One would think that the solution springs suddenly from the very enunciation of the problem, in the same way as a veridical hallucination. It appears to rise, infallible and ready-done, from a sort of eternal and cosmic reservoir wherein the answers to every question lie dormant. It must, therefore, be admitted that we have here a phenomenon that occurs above or below the brain, by the side of the consciousness and the mind, outside all the intellectual methods and habits; and it is precisely for phenomena of this kind that Myers invented the word "subliminal."[1]

[1] I have no need to recall the derivation of the term subliminal: beneath (*sub*) the threshold (*limen*) of consciousness. Let us add, as M. de Vesme very rightly remarks, that the subliminal is not exactly what classical psychology calls the subconsciousness, which latter records only notions that are normally perceived and possesses only normal faculties, that is to say, faculties recognized to-day by orthodox science.

32

Does not all this bring us a little nearer to our calculating horses? From the moment that it is demonstrated that the solution of a mathematical problem no longer depends exclusively on the brain, but on another faculty, another spiritual power whose presence under various forms has been ascertained beyond a doubt in certain animals, it ceases to be wholly rash or extravagant to suggest that perhaps, in the horse, the same phenomenon is reproduced and developed in the same unknown, wherein moreover the mysteries of numbers and those of subconsciousness mingle in a like darkness. I am well aware that an explanation laden to such an extent with mysteries explains but very little more than silence does; nevertheless, it is at least a silence traversed by restless murmurs and sedulous whispers that are better than the gloomy and hopeless ignorance to which we would have perforce to resign ourselves if we did not struggle, in spite of all, to perform the great duty of man, which is to discover a spark in the darkness.

It goes without saying that objections are raised from every side. Among men, arithmetical prodigies are looked upon as monsters, as a sort of extremely rare teratological phenomenon. We can count, at most, half-a-dozen in a century, whereas, among horses, the faculty would appear to be almost general, or at least quite common. In fact, out of six or seven stallions whom Krall tried to initiate into the secrets of mathematics, he found only two that appeared to him too poorly gifted for him to waste time on their education. These were, I believe, two thoroughbreds that were presented to him by the Grand-duke of Mecklenburg and sent back by Krall to their sumptuous stables. In the four or five others, taken at random as circumstances supplied them, he met with aptitudes unequal, it is true, but easily developed and giving the impression that they exist normally, latent and inactive, at the bottom of every equine soul. From the mathematical point of view, is the horse's subliminal consciousness then superior to man's? Why not? His whole subliminal being is probably superior to ours, of greater range, younger, fresher, more alive and less heavy, since it is not incessantly attacked, coerced and humiliated by the intelligence which gnaws at it, stifles it, cloaks it and relegates it to a dark corner which neither light nor air can penetrate. His subliminal consciousness is always present, always alert; ours is never there, is asleep at the bottom of a deserted well and needs exceptional operations, results and events before it can be drawn from its slumber and its unremembered deeps. All this seems very extraordinary; but, in any case, we are here

338

in the midst of the extraordinary; and this
outlet is perhaps the least hazardous. It
is not a question, we must remember, of a
cerebral operation, an intellectual performance, but of a gift of divination closely al-
lied to other gifts of the same nature and
the same origin which are not the peculiar
attribute of man. No observation, no experiment enables us, up to the present, to
establish a difference between the subliminal
of human beings and that of animals. On
the contrary, the as yet restricted number
of actual cases reveals constant and striking
analogies between the two. In most of
those arithmetical operations, be it noted,
the subliminal of the horse behaves exactly
like that of the medium in a state of trance.
The horse readily reverses the figures of
the solution; he replies, "37," for instance,
instead of "73," which is a mediumistic
phenomenon so well-known and so frequent
that it has been styled "mirror-writing."

339

He makes mistakes fairly often in the most elementary additions and subtractions and much less frequently in the extraction of the most complicated roots, which again, in similar cases, such as "xenoglossy" and psychometry, is one of the eccentricities of human mediumism and is explained by the same cause, namely, the inopportune intervention of the ever fallible intelligence, which, by meddling in the matter, alters the certainties of a subliminal which, when left to itself, never makes a mistake. It is, in fact, quite probable that the horse, being really able to do the small sums, no longer relies solely on his intuition and, from that moment, gropes and flounders about. The solution hovers between the intelligence and the subliminal and, passing from the one, which is not quite sure of it, to the other, which is not urgently appealed to, comes out of the conflict as best it may. The case is the same with the psychometric or

spiritualistic medium who seeks to profit by
what he knows in the ordinary way, so as
to complete the visions or revelations of his
subconscious sensibility. He, too, in this
instance, is nearly always guilty of flagrant
and inexplicable blunders.

Many other similarities will be found to
exist, notably the way in which the lessons
vary. Nothing is more uncertain and capricious than manifestations of human mediumism. Whether it be a question of automatic writing, psychometry, materializations or anything else, we meet with series
of sittings that yield none but absurd results. Then, suddenly, for reasons as yet
obscure—the state of the weather, the presence of this or that witness, or I know not
what—the most undeniable and bewildering
manifestations occur one after the other.
The case is precisely the same with the
horses: their queer fancies, their unaccount-
able and disconcerting freaks drive poor

Krall to despair. He never opens the door of that uncertain stable, on important days, without a sinking at the heart. Let the beard or the frown of some learned professor fail to please the horses: they will, forthwith, take an unholy delight in giving the most irrelevant answers to the most elementary questions for hours and even days on end.

Other common features are the strongly-marked personality of the mediumistic "raps" and the communications known as "deferred telepathic communications," that is to say, those in which the answer is obtained at the end of a sitting to a question put at the beginning and forgotten by all those present. What at first sight seems one of the strongest objections urged against the mediumism of the horse even tends to confirm it. If the reply comes from the horse's subconsciousness, it has been asked, how is it that it should be necessary

342

first to teach him the elements of language,
mathematics and so forth, and that Berto,
for instance, is incapable of solving the
same problems as Muhamed? This objection has been very ably refuted by M. de
Vesme, who writes:

"To produce automatic writing, a medium must have learnt to write; before
Victorien Sardou or Mlle Hélène Schmidt
could produce their mediumistic drawings
and paintings, they had to possess an elementary knowledge of drawing and painting; Tartini would never have composed
The Devil's Sonata in a dream, if he had
not known music; and so forth. Unconscious cerebration, however wonderful, can
only take effect upon elements already acquired in some way or another. The subconscious cerebration of a man blind from
birth will not make him see colours."

Here, then, in this comparison which might easily be extended, are several fairly well-defined features of resemblance. We receive a vivid impression of the same habits, the same contradictions and the same eccentricities; and we once more recognize the strange and majestic shadow of our unknown guest.

33

One great objection remains, based upon the very nature of the phenomenon, upon the really insuperable distance that separates the whole life of the horse from the abstract and impenetrable life of numbers. How can his subliminal consciousness interest itself for a moment in signs that represent nothing to him, have no relation to his organism and will never touch his existence? But, in the first place, it is just the same with the child or the illiterate calculator. He is not interested either in the figures which he lets loose. He is completely ignorant of the consequences of the problems which he solves. He juggles with digits which have hardly any more meaning to him than to the horse. He is incapable of accounting for what he does; and his subconsciousness also acts in a sort of indifferent and remote dream. It is true that, in his case, we can appeal to heredity and to memory; but is this difference enough to settle the difficulty and definitely to separate the two phenomena? To appeal to heredity is still to appeal to the subliminal; and it is not at all certain that the latter is limited by the interest of the organism sheltering it. It appears, on the contrary, in many circumstances, to spread and extend far beyond that organism in which it is domiciled, one would say, accidentally and provisionally. It likes to show, apparently, that it is in relation with all

345

that exists. It declares itself, as often as possible, universal and impersonal. It has but a very indifferent care, as we have seen in the matter of apparitions and premonitions, for the happiness and even the safety of its host and protector. It prophesies to its companion of a lifetime events which he cannot avoid or which do not concern him. It makes him see beforehand, for instance, all the circumstances of the death of a stranger whom he will only hear of after the event, when this event is irrevocable. It brings a crowd of barren presentiments and conjures up veridical hallucinations that are wholly alien and idle. With psychometric, typtological or materializing mediums, it practises art for art's sake, mocks at space and time, passes through personalities, sees through solid bodies, brings into communication thoughts and emotions worlds apart, reads souls and lives by the light of a flower, a rag or a scrap of paper; and all this for nothing, to amuse itself, to astonish us, because it adores the superfluous, the incoherent, the unexpected, the improbable, the bewildering, or rather, perhaps, because it is a huge, rough, undisciplined force still struggling in the darkness and coming to the surface only by wild fits and starts, because it is an enormous expansion of a spirit striving to collect itself, to achieve consciousness, to make itself of service and to obtain a hearing. In any case, for the time being, it appears just what we have described, and would be unlike itself if it behaved any otherwise in the case that puzzles us.

34

Lastly, to close this chapter, let us remark that it is nearly certain that the solution given by calculating children and horses is not of a mathematical nature at all. They do not in any way consider the problem or the sum to be worked. They simply find the answer straight away to a riddle, the guessing of which is made easy by the actual nature of figures which keep their secrets badly. To any one in the requisite state of mind, it becomes a question of a sort of elementary charade, which hides its answer only from those who speak another language. It is evident that every problem, however complex it may appear, carries within its very enunciation its one, invariable solution, scarce veiled by the indiscreet signs that contain or cover it. It is there, under the numbers that have no other object than to give it life, tossing, stirring and ceaselessly proclaiming itself a necessity. It is not surprising therefore that eyes sharper than ours and ears open to other vibrations should see and hear it without knowing what it represents, what it implies or from what prodigious mass of figures and operations it emerges. The problem itself speaks; and the horse but repeats the sign which he hears whispered in the mysterious life of numbers or deep down in the abyss where the eternal verities hold sway. He understands none of it, he has no need to understand, he is but the unconscious medium who lends his voice or his limbs to the mind that inspires him. There is here but a bare and simple answer, bearing no precise significance, seized in an alien existence. There is here but a mechanical revelation, so to speak, a sort of special reflex which we can only record and which, for the rest, is as inexplicable as any other phenomenon of consciousness or instinct. After all, when we think of it, it is just as astonishing that we should not perceive the solution as it is that we should discover it. However, I grant that all this is but a venturesome interpretation to be taken for what it is worth, an experimental or interim theory with which we must needs content

ourselves since all the others have hitherto
been controverted by the facts.

35

Let us now briefly sum up what these
Elberfeld experiments have yielded us.
Having put aside telepathy in the narrow
sense—which perhaps enters into more
than one phenomenon but is not indispensable to it, for we see these same phenomena repeated when telepathy is practically impossible—we cannot help observing that, if we deny the existence or the
influence of the subliminal, it is all the more
difficult to contest the existence and the intervention of the intelligence, at any rate up
to the extracting of roots, after which there
is a steep precipice which ends in darkness.
But, even if we stop at the roots, the sudden
discovery of an intellectual force so similar
to our own, where we were accustomed to
see but an irremediable impotency, is no

doubt one of the most unexpected revelations that we have received since the invisible and the unknown began to press upon us with a persistence and an impatience which they had not displayed heretofore. It is not easy to foresee as yet the consequences and the promises of this new aspect which the great riddle of the intelligence is suddenly adopting. But I believe that we shall soon have to revise some of the essential ideas which are the foundations of our life and that some rather strange horizons are appearing out of the mists in the history of psychology, of morality, of human destiny and of many other things.

36

So much for the intelligence. On the other hand, what we deny to the intelligence we are constrained to grant to the subliminal; and the revelation is even more disconcerting. We should then have to admit that there is in the horse—and hence most probably in everything that lives on this earth—a psychic power similar to that which is hidden beneath the veil of our reason and which, as we learn to know it, astonishes, surpasses and dominates our reason more and more. This psychic power, in which no doubt we shall one day be forced to recognize the genius of the universe itself, appears, as we have often observed, to be all-wise, all-seeing and all-powerful. It has, when it is pleased to communicate with us or when we are allowed to penetrate into it, an answer for every question and perhaps a remedy for every ill. We will not enumerate its virtues again. It will be enough for us to recall with what ease it mocks at space, time and all the obstacles that beset our poor human knowledge and understanding. We believed it, like all that seems to us superior and marvellous, the intangible, inalienable and incommunicable attribute of man, with even better reason than his intelligence. And now an accident, strangely belated, it is true, tells us that, at one precise point, the strangest and least foreseen of all, the horse and the dog draw more easily and perhaps more directly than ourselves upon its mighty reservoirs. By the most inexplicable of anomalies, though one that is fairly consistent with the fantastic character of the subliminal, they appear to have access to it only at the spot that is most remote from their habits and most unknown to their propensities, for there is nothing in the world about which animals trouble less than figures. But is this not perhaps because we do not see what goes on elsewhere? It so happens that the infinite mystery of numbers can sometimes be expressed by a very few simple movements which are natural to most animals;

but there is nothing to tell us that, if we could teach the horse and the dog to attach to these same movements the expression of other mysteries, they would not draw upon them with equal facility. It has been successfully attempted to give them a more or less clear idea of the value of a few figures and perhaps of the course and nature of certain elementary operations; and this appears to have been enough to open up to them the most secret regions of mathematics, in which every question is answered beforehand. It is not wholly illusive to suppose that, if we could impart to them, for instance, a similar notion of the future, together with a manner of conveying to us what they see there, they might also have access to strange visions of another class, which are jealously kept from us by the too-watchful guardians of our intelligence. There is an opportunity here for experiments which will doubtless prove

354

exceedingly arduous, for the future is not so easily seen and above all not so easily interpreted and expressed as a number. It is possible, moreover, that, when we know how to set about it, we shall obtain most of the human mediumistic phenomena: rapping, the moving of objects, materialization even and Heaven knows what other surprises held in store for us by that astounding subliminal to whose fancy there appears to be no bounds. In any case, if we accept the divining of numbers, as we are almost forced to do, it is almost certain that the divining of other matters must follow. An unexpected breach is made in the wall behind which lie heaped the great secrets that seem to us, as our knowledge and our civilization increase, to become stronger and more inaccessible. True, it is a narrow breach; but it is the first that has been opened in that part of the hitherto uncrannied wall which is not turned towards man-

kind. What will issue through it? No one
can foretell what we may hope.

37

What astonishes us most is that this revelation has been so long delayed. How are
we to explain that man has lived to this day
with his domestic animals never suspecting
that they harboured mediumistic or subliminal faculties as extraordinary as those
which he vaguely felt himself to possess?
One would have in this connection to study
the mysterious practices of ancient India
and of Egypt; the numerous and persistent
legends of animals talking, guiding their
masters and foretelling the future; and,
nearer to ourselves, in history proper, all
that science of augury and soothsaying
which derived its omens from the flight of
birds, the inspection of entrails, the appetite or attitude of the sacred or prophetic
animals, among which horses were often

numbered. We here find one of those innumerous instances of a lost or anticipated
power which make us suspect that mankind has forestalled or forgotten all that
we believe ourselves to be discovering. Remember that there is almost always some
distorted, misapprehended or dimly-seen
truth at the bottom of the most eccentric
and wildest creeds, superstitions and legends. All this new science of metaphysics
or of the investigation of our subconsciousness and of unknown powers, which has
scarcely begun to unveil its first mysteries,
thus finds landmarks and defaced but recog-
nizable traces in the old religions, the most
inexplicable traditions and the most ancient
history. Besides, the probability of a thing
does not depend upon undeniably established precedents. While it is almost certain that there is nothing new under the
sun or in the eternity preceding the suns,
it is quite possible that the same forces do

not always act with the same energy. As I observed, nearly twenty years ago, in *The Treasure of the Humble,* at a time when I hardly knew at all what I know so imperfectly to-day:

"A spiritual"—I should have said, a psychic—"epoch is perhaps upon us, an epoch to which a certain number of analogies are found in history. For there are periods recorded when the soul, in obedience to unknown laws, seemed to rise to the very surface of humanity, whence it gave clearest evidence of its existence and of its power. . . . It would seem, at moments such as these, as though humanity"—and, I would add to-day, all that lives with it on this earth—"were on the point of struggling from beneath the crushing burden of matter that weighs it down."

One might in fact believe that a shudder which we have not yet experienced is pass-

ing over everything that breathes; that a
new activity, a new restlessness is permeating the spiritual atmosphere which surrounds our globe; and that the very animals have felt its thrill. One might say
that, by the side of the niggardly private
spring which would only supply our intelligence, other streams are spreading and rising to the same level in every form of existence. A sort of word of command is being
passed from rank to rank; and the same
phenomena are bursting forth in every
quarter of the globe in order to attract our
attention, as though the obstinately dumb
genius that lay hidden in the pregnant silence of the universe, from that of the
stones, the flowers and the insects to the
mighty silence of the stars, were at last
trying to tell us some secret whereby it
would be better known to us or to itself. It
is possible that this is but an illusion. Perhaps we are simply more attentive and bet-

ter informed than of old. We learn at the very instant what happens in every part of our earth and we have acquired the habit of more minutely observing and examining the things that happen. But the illusion would in this case have all the force, all the value and all the meaning of the reality and would enjoin the same hopes and the same obligations.

CHAPTER V
THE UNKNOWN GUEST

CHAPTER V

THE UNKNOWN GUEST

I

WE have now studied certain manifestations of that which we have called in turn and more or less indiscriminately the subconscious mind, the subliminal consciousness and the unknown guest, names to which we might add that of the superior subconsciousness or superior psychism invented by Dr. Geley. Granting that these manifestations are really proved, it is no longer possible to explain them or rather to classify them without having recourse to fresh theories. Now we can entertain doubts on many points, we can cavil and argue; but I defy any one approaching these facts in a serious and honest spirit to reject them all. It is permissible to neglect the most extraordinary; but there are a multitude of others which have become or, to speak more accurately, are acknowledged to be as frequent and habitual as any fact whatever in normal, everyday life. It is not difficult to reproduce them at will, provided we place ourselves in the condition demanded by their very nature; and, this being so, there remains no valid reason for excluding them from the domain of science in the strict sense of the word.

Hitherto, all that we have learnt regarding these occurrences is that their origin is unknown. It will be said that this is not much and that the discovery is nothing to boast of. I quite agree: to imagine that one can explain a phenomena by saying that it is produced by an unknown agency would indeed be childish. But it is already something to have marked its source, not to be still lingering in the thick of a fog, trying any and every direction in order to find a way out, but to be concentrating our attention on a single spot which is the starting-point of all these wonders, so that at each instant we recognize in each phenomenon the characteristic customs, methods or features of the same unknown agency. It is very nearly all that we can do for the moment; but this first effort is not wholly to be despised.

2

It has seemed to us then that it was our unknown guest that expressed itself in the name of the dead in table-turning and in automatic writing and speaking. This unknown guest has appeared to us to take within us the place of those who are no more, to unite itself perhaps with forces that do not die, to visit the grave with the object of bringing thence inexplicable phantoms which rise up in front of us fruitlessly or haunt our houses without telling us why. We have seen it, in experiments in clairvoyance and intuition, suppressing all the obstacles that banish or conceal thought and, through bodies that have become transparent, reading in our very souls forgotten secrets of the past, sentiments that have not yet taken shape, intentions as yet unborn. We have discovered that some object once handled by a person now far away is enough to make it take part in the innermost life of that person, to go deeper and rise higher than he does, to see what he sees and even what he does not see: the landscape that surrounds him, the house which he inhabits and also the dangers that threaten him and the secret passions by which he is stirred. We have surprised it wandering hither and thither, at haphazard, in the future, confounding it with the present and the past, not conscious of where it is but seeing far and wide, knowing perhaps everything but unaware of the importance of what it knows, or as yet incapable of turning it to account or of making itself understood, at once neglectful and overscrupulous, prolix and reticent, useless and indispensable. We have seen it, lastly, although we had hitherto looked upon it as indissolubly and unchangeably human, suddenly emerge from other creatures and there reveal faculties akin to ours, which commune with them deep down in the deepest mysteries and which equal them and sometimes surpass them in a region that wrongly appeared to us the only really unassailable province of mankind, I mean the obscure and abstruse province of numbers.

It has many other no less strange and perhaps more important manifestations, which we propose to examine in a later volume, notably its surprising therapeutic virtues and its phenomena of materialization. But, without expressing a premature judgment on what we do not yet know, perhaps we have sketched it with sufficient clearness in the foregoing pages to enable us henceforward to disentangle certain general and characteristic features from a confusion of often contradictory lines.

3

But, in the first place, does it really exist, this tragic and comical, evasive and unavoidable figure which we make no claim to portray, but at most to divest of some of its shadows? It were rash to affirm it too loudly; but meanwhile, in the realms where we suppose it to reign, everything happens as though it did exist. Do away with it and you are obliged to people the world and burden your life with a host of hypothetical and imaginary beings: gods, demigods, angels, demons, saints, spirits, shells, elementals, etherial entities, interplanetary intelligences and so on; accept it and all those phantoms, without disappearing, for they may very well continue to live in its shadow, become superfluous or accessory. It is not intolerant and does not definitely eliminate any of the hypotheses by the aid of which man has hitherto striven to explain what he did not understand, hypotheses which, in regard to some matters, are not inadmissible, although not one of them is confirmed; but it brings them back to itself, absorbs them and rules them without annihilating them. If, for instance, to select the most defensible theory, one which it is sometimes difficult to dismiss absolutely, if you insist that the discarnate spirits take part in your actions, haunt your house, inspire your thoughts, reveal your future, it will answer:

"That is true, but it is still I; I am discarnate, or rather I am not wholly incarnate:it is only a small part of my being that is embodied in your flesh; and the rest, which is nearly all of me, comes and goes freely both among those who once were and among those who are yet to be; and, when they seem to speak to you, it is my own speech that borrows their customs and their voice in order to make you listen and to arouse your often slumbering attention. If you prefer to deal with superior entities of unknown origin, with interplanetary or supernatural intelligences, once more it is I; for, since I am not entirely in your body, I must needs be elsewhere; and to be elsewhere when one is not held back by the weight of the flesh is to be everywhere if one so pleases."

We see, it has a reply to everything, it takes every name that we wish and there is nothing to limit it, because it lives in a world wherein bounds are as illusory as the useless words which we employ on earth.

4

While it has a reply to everything, certain manifestations which it deliberately ascribes to the spirits have brought upon it grave and not undeserved reproach. To begin with, as Dr. Maxwell observes, it has no absolutely fixed doctrine. In nearly every country in the world, when it speaks in the name of the spirits, it declares that they undergo reincarnation and readily relates their past existences. In England, on the contrary, it usually asserts that they do not become reincarnated. What does this mean? Surely this ignorance or this inconsistency on the part of that which appears to know everything is very strange! And worse, sometimes it attributes to the spirits, sometimes to itself or any one or anything the revelations which it makes to us. When exactly is it speaking the truth? At least on two occasions out of three, it deludes itself or deludes us. If it deceives itself, if it is mistaken about a matter in which it should be easy for it to know the truth, what can it teach us on the subject of a world of whose most elementary laws it is ignorant, since it does not even know whether it is itself or another that speaks to us in the name of that world? Are we to believe that it moves in the same darkness as our poor superficial ego, which it pretends so often to enlighten and which it does in fact inspire in most of the great events of life? If it deceives us, why does it do so? We can see no object: it asks for nothing, not for alms, nor prayers, nor thoughts, on behalf of those whose mantle it assumes for the sole purpose of leading us astray. What is the use of those mischievous and puerile pranks, of those ghastly graveyard pleasantries? It must lie then for the mere pleasure of lying; and our unknown guest, that infinite and doubtless immortal subconsciousness in which we have placed our last hopes, is after all but an imbecile, a buffoon or a rank swindler!

The Unknown Guest

5

I do not believe that the truth is as hideous as this. Our unknown guest does not deceive itself any more than it deceives us; but it is we who deceive ourselves. It has not the stage to itself; and its voice is not the voice that sounds in our ears, which were never made to catch the echoes of a world that is not like ours. If it could speak to us itself and tell us what it knows, we should probably at that instant cease to be on this earth. But we are immured in our bodies, entombed prisoners with whom it cannot communicate at will. It roams around the walls, it utters warning cries, it knocks at every door, but all that reaches us is a vague disquiet, an indistinct murmur that is sometimes translated to us by a half-awakened gaoler who, like ourselves, is a lifelong captive. The gaoler does his best; he has his own way of speaking, his familiar expressions; he knows ours and, with the aid of the words which he possesses and those which he hears repeated, he tries to make us understand what he hardly understands himself. He does not know exactly whence the sounds come which he hears; and, according as tempests, wars or riots happen to be uppermost at the moment, he attributes them to the winds, to tramping soldiers or to frenzied crowds. In other words and speaking without metaphor, it is the medium who draws from his habitual language and from that suggested to him by his audience the wherewithal to clothe and identify the strange presentiments, the unfamiliar visions that come from some unknown region. If he believes that the dead survive, he will naturally imagine that it is the dead who speak to him. If he has a favourite spirit, angel, demon or god, he will express himself in its name; if he has no preconceived opinion, he will not even allude to the origin of the revelations which

he is making. The inarticulate language
of the subconsciousness necessarily borrows
that of the normal consciousness; and the
two become confused into a sort of shifting
and multiform jargon. And our unknown
guest, which is not thinking of delivering a
course of lectures upon its entity, but simply giving us as best it can a more or less
useless warning or a mark of its existence,
seems to care but little as to the garments
in which it is rigged out, having indeed no
choice in the matter, for, either because it
is unable to manifest itself or because we
are incapable of understanding it, it has to
be content with whatever comes to hand.

Besides, if we attribute too exclusively to
the spirits that which comes from another
quarter, the mistake is doubtless no great
one in its eyes; for it is not madness to
believe that it lives with that which does
not die in the dead even as with that which
does not die in ourselves, with that which

does not descend into the grave even as with that which does not take flesh at the hour of birth.

6

There is no reason therefore to condemn the other theories entirely. Most of them doubtless contain something more than a particle of truth; in particular, the great quarrel between the subconscious school and the spiritualists is based on the whole upon a misunderstanding. It is quite possible and even very probable that the dead are all around us, since it is impossible that the dead do not live. Our subconsciousness must mingle with all that does not die in them; and that which dies in them or rather disperses and loses all its importance is but the little consciousness accumulated on this earth and kept up until the last hour by the frail bonds of memory. In all those manifestations of our unknown guest, it is our posthumous ego that already lives in us while we are still in the flesh and at moments joins that which does not die in those who have quitted their body. Then does the existence of our unknown guest presume the immortality of a part of ourselves? Can one possibly doubt it? Have you ever imagined that you would perish entirely? As for me, what I cannot picture is the manner in which you would picture that total annihilation. But, if you cannot perish entirely, it is no less certain that those who came before you have not perished either; and hence it is not altogether improbable that we may be able to discover them and to communicate with them. In this wider sense, the spiritualistic theory is perfectly admissible; but what is not at all admissible is the narrow and pitiful interpretation which its exponents too often give it. They see the dead crowding around us like wretched puppets indissolubly attached to the insignificant scene of their death by the thousand little threads of insipid memories and infantile hobbies. They are supposed to be here, blocking up our homes, more abjectly human than if they were still alive, vague, inconsistent, garrulous, derelict, futile and idle, tossing hither and thither their desolate shadows, which are being slowly swallowed up by silence and oblivion, busying themselves incessantly with what no longer concerns them, but almost incapable of doing us a real service, so much so that, in short, they would end by persuading us that death serves no purpose, that it neither purifies nor exalts, that it brings no deliverance and that it is indeed a thing of terror and despair.

7

No, it is not the dead who thus speak and act. Besides, why bring them into the matter unnecessarily? I could understand that we should be obliged to do so if there were no similar phenomena outside them; but in the intuition and clairvoyance of non-spiritualistic mediums and particularly in psychometry we obtain communications between one subconsciousness and another and revelations of unknown, forgotten or future incidents which are equally striking, though stripped of the vapid gossip and tedious reminiscences with which we are overwhelmed by defunct persons who are all the more jealous to prove their identity inasmuch as they know that they do not exist.

It is infinitely more likely that there is a strange medley of heterogeneous forces in the uncertain regions into which we are venturing. The whole of this ambiguous drama, with its incoherent crowds, is probably enacted round about the dim estuary where our normal consciousness flows into our subconsciousness. The consciousness of the medium—for we must not forget that there is necessarily always a medium at the sources of these phenomena—the consciousness of the medium, obscured by the condition of trance but yet the only one that possesses our human speech and can make itself heard, takes in first and almost exclusively what it best understands and what most interests it in the stifled and mutilated revelations of our unknown guest, which for its part communicates with the dead and the living and everything that exists. The rest, which is the only thing that matters, but which is less clear and less vivid because it comes from afar, only very rarely makes its difficult way through a forest of insignificant talk. We may add that our subconsciousness, as Dr. Geley very rightly observes, is formed of superposed elements, beginning with the unconsciousness that governs the instinctive movements of the organic life of both the species and the individual and passing by imperceptible degrees till it rises to the superior psychism whose power and extent appear to have no bounds. The voice of the medium, or that which we hear within ourselves when, at certain moments of excitement or crisis in our lives, we become our own medium, has therefore to traverse three worlds or three provinces: that of the atavistic instincts which connect us with the animal; that of human or empirical consciousness; and lastly that of our unknown guest or our superior subconsciousness, which links us to immense invisible realities and which we may, if we wish, call divine or superhuman. Hence it is not surprising that the intermediary, be he spiritualist, autonomist, palingenesist or what he will, should lose himself in those wild and troubled eddies and that the truth or message which he brings us, tossed and tumbled in every direction, should reach us broken, shattered and pulverized beyond recognition.

For the rest, I repeat, were it not for the absurd prominence given to our dead in the spiritualistic interpretation, this question of origin would have little importance, since both life and death are incessantly joining and uniting in all things. There are assuredly dead people in all these manifestations, seeing that we are full of dead people and that the greater part of ourselves is at this moment steeped in death, that is to say, is already living the boundless life that awaits us on the farther side of the grave.

8

We should be wrong, however, to fix all our attention on these extraordinary phenomena, either those with which we unduly connect the deceased or those no less striking ones in which we do not believe that they take part. They are evidently precious points of emergence that enable us approximately to mark the extent, the forms and the habits of our mystery. But it is within ourselves, in the silence of the darkness of our being, where it is ever in motion, guiding our destiny, that we should strive to surprise that mystery and to discover it. And I am not speaking only of the dreams, the presentiments, the vague intuitions, the more or less brilliant inspirations which are so many more manifestations, specific as it were and analogous with those that have occupied us. There is another, a more secret and much more active existence which we have scarcely begun to study and which is, if we descend to the bed-rock of truth, our only real existence. From the darkest corners of our ego it directs our veritable life, the one that is not to die, and pays no heed to our thought or to anything emanating from our reason, which believes that it guides our steps. It alone knows the long past that preceded our birth and the endless future that will follow our departure from this earth. It is itself that future and that past, all those from whom we have sprung and all those who will spring from us. It represents in the individual not only the species but that which preceded it and that which will follow it; and it has neither beginning nor end: that is why nothing touches it, nothing moves it which does not concern that which it represents. When a misfortune or a joy befall us, it knows their value instantly, knows if they are going to open or to close the wells of life. It is the one thing that is never wrong. In vain does reason demonstrate to it, by irresistible arguments, that it is hopelessly at fault: silent under its immovable mask, whose expression we have not yet been able to read, it pursues its way. It treats us as insignificant children, void of understanding, never answers our objections, refuses what we ask and lavishes upon us that which we refuse.

The Unknown Guest

If we go to the right, it reconducts us to the
left. If we cultivate this or that faculty
which we think that we possess or which we
would like to possess, it hides it under some
other which we did not expect and did not
wish for. It saves us from a danger by im-
parting to our limbs unforeseen and unerr-
ing movements and actions which they had
never made before and which are contrary
to those which they had been taught to
make: it knows that the hour has not yet
come when it will be useless to defend ourselves. It chooses our love in spite of the
revolt of our intelligence or of our poor,
ephemeral heart. It smiles when we are
frightened and sometimes it is frightened
when we smile. And it is always the win-
ner, humiliating our reason, crushing our
wisdom and silencing arguments and passions alike with the contemptuous hand of
destiny. The greatest doctors surround
our sick-bed and deceive themselves and us

in foretelling our death or our recovery: it alone whispers in our ear the truth that will not be denied. A thousand apparently mortal blows fall upon our head and not a lash of its eyelids quivers; but suddenly a tiny shock, which our senses had not even transmitted to our brain, wakes it with a start. It sits up, looks around and understands. It has seen the crack in the vault that separates the two lives. It gives the signal for departure. Forthwith panic spreads from cell to cell; and the innumerous city that we are utters yells of horror and distress and hustles around the gates of death.

9

That great figure, that new being has been there, in our darkness, from all time, though its awkward and extravagant actions, until recently attributed to the gods, the demons or the dead, are only now asking for our serious attention. It has been

386

likened to an immense block of which our personality is but a diminutive facet; to an iceberg of which we see a few glistening prisms that represent our life, while nine-tenths of the enormous mass remain buried in the shadows of the sea. According to Sir Oliver Lodge, it is that part of our being that has not become carnate; according to Gustave Le Bon, it is the "condensed" soul of our ancestors, which is true, beyond a doubt, but only a part of the truth, for we find in it also the soul of the future and probably of many other forces which are not necessarily human. William James saw in it a diffuse cosmic consciousness and the chance intrusion into our scientifically-organized world of remnants and bestiges of the primordial chaos. Here are a number of images striving to give us an idea of a reality so vast that we are unable to grasp it. It is certain that what we see from our terrestrial life is nothing compared with what we do not see. Besides, if we think of it, it would be monstrous and inexplicable that we should be only what we appear to be, nothing but ourselves, whole and complete in ourselves, separated, isolated, circumscribed by our body, our mind, our consciousness, our birth and our death. We become possible and probable only on the conditions that we project beyond ourselves on every side and that we stretch in every direction throughout time and space.

10

But how shall we explain the incredible contrast between the immeasurable grandeur of our unknown guest, the assurance, the calmness, the gravity of the inner life which it leads in us and the puerile and sometimes grotesque incongruities of what one might call its public existence? Inside us, it is the sovereign judge, the supreme

arbiter, the prophet, almost the god omni-
potent; outside us, from the moment that
it quits its shelter and manifests itself in
external actions, it is nothing more than a
fortune-teller, a bone-setter, a sort of facetious conjuror or telephone-operator, I was
on the verge of saying a mountebank or
clown. At what particular instant is it
really itself? Is it seized with giddiness
when it leaves its lair? Is it we who no
longer hear it, who no longer understand it,
as soon as it ceases to speak in a whisper
and to act in the dark recesses of our life?
Are we in regard to it the terrified hive in-
vaded by a huge and inexplicable hand, the
maddened ant-hill trampled by a colossal
and incomprehensible foot? Let us not
venture yet to solve the strange riddle with
the aid of the little that we know. Let us
confine ourselves, for the moment, to noting
on the way some other, rather easier questions which we can at least try to answer.

The Unknown Guest

First of all, are the facts at issue really new? Was it only yesterday that the existence of our unknown guest and its external manifestations were revealed to us? Is it our attention that makes them appear more numerous, or is it the increase in their number that at last attracts our attention?

It does indeed seem that, however far we go back in history, we everywhere find the same extraordinary phenomena, under other names and often in a more glamorous setting. Oracles, prophecies, incantations, haruspication, "possession," evocation of the dead, apparitions, ghosts, miraculous cures, levitation, transmission of thought, apparent resurrections and the rest are the exact equivalent, though magnified by the aid of plentiful and obvious frauds of our latter-day supernaturalism. Turning in another direction, we are able to see that psychical phenomena are very evenly distributed over the whole surface of the globe.

The Unknown Guest

At all events, there does not appear to be any race that is absolutely or peculiarly refractory to them. One would be inclined to say, however, that they manifest themselves by preference among the most civilized nations—perhaps because that is where they are most carefully sought after —and among the most primitive. In short, it cannot be denied that we are in the presence of faculties or senses, more or less latent but at the same time universally distributed, which form part of the general and unvarying inheritance of mankind. But have these faculties or senses undergone evolution, like most of the others? And, if they have not done so on our earth, do they show traces of an extraplanetary evolution? Is there progress or reaction? Are they withered and useless branches, or buds swollen with sap and promise? Are they retreating before the march of intelligence or invading its domain?

II

M. Ernest Bozzano, one of the most learned, most daring and most subtle exponents of the new science that is in process of formation, in the course of a remarkable essay in the *Annales des sciences psychiques*,[1] gives it as his opinion that they have remained stationary and unchanged. He considers that they have become in no way diffused, generalized and refined, like so many others that are much less important and useful from the point of view of the struggle for life, such as the musical faculty, for instance. It does not even seem, says M. Bozzano, that it is possible to cultivate or develop them systematically. The Hindu races in particular, who for thousands of years have been devoting themselves to the study of these manifestations, have arrived at nothing but a better knowledge of the empirical methods cal-

[1] September 1906.

culated to produce them in individuals already endowed with these supernormal faculties. I do not know to what extent M. Bozzano's assertions are beyond dispute. They concern historical or remote facts which it is very difficult to verify. In any case, it is something to have perfected, as has been done in India, the empirical methods favourable to the production of supernormal phenomena. One might even say that it is about all that we have the right to expect, seeing that, by the author's own admission, these faculties are latent in every man and that, as has frequently been seen, it needs but an illness, a lesion, or sometimes even the slightest emotion or a mere passing faintness to make them suddenly reveal themselves in an individual who seemed most hopelessly devoid of them. It is therefore quite possible that, by improving the methods, by attacking the mystery from other quarters, we might obtain more decisive results than the Hindus. We must remember that our western science has but lately interested itself in these problems and that it has means of investigating and experimenting which the Asiatics never possessed. It may even be declared that at no time in the existence of our world has the scientific mind been better-equipped, better-suited to cope with every task, or more exact, more skilful and more penetrating than it is to-day. Because the oriental empirics have failed, there is no reason to believe that it will not succeed in awakening and cultivating in every man those faculties which would often be of greater use to him than those of the intellect itself. It is not overbold to suggest that, from certain points of view, the true history of mankind has hardly begun.

12

Nevertheless, in so far as concerns the

natural evolution of those faculties, M. Bozzano's assertion seems fairly well-justified. We do not, in fact, observe a startling or even appreciable difference between what they were and what they are. And this anomaly is the more surprising in as much as it is almost universally accepted that a sense or a faculty becomes developed in proportion to its usefulness; and there are few, I think, that would have been not only more useful but even more necessary to man. He has always had a keen and primitive interest in knowing without delay the most secret thoughts of his fellow-man, who is often his adversary and sometimes his mortal enemy. He has always had an interest no less great in immediately transmitting those thoughts through space, in seeing beyond the continents and seas, in going back into the past, in advancing into the future, in being able to find in his memory at will not only all the acquirements of his personal experience but also those of his ancestors, in communicating with the dead and perhaps with the sovereign intelligence diffused over the universe, in discovering hidden springs and treasures, in escaping the harsh and depressing laws of matter and gravity, in relieving pain, in curing the greater number of his disorders and even in restoring his limbs, not to mention many other miracles which he could work if he knew all the mighty forces that doubtless slumber in the dark recesses of his life.

Is this once more an unexpected character of the eccentric physiology of our unknown guest? Here are faculties more precious than the most precious faculties that have made us what we are, faculties whose magic buds sprout on every side underneath our intelligence but have never burst into flower, as though a wind from another sphere had killed them with its icy breath. Is it because it occupies itself first and foremost with the species that it thus neglects the individual? But, after all, the species is only an aggregate of successive individuals; and its evolution consequently depends upon their evolution. There would therefore have been an evident advantage to the species in developing faculties that would perhaps have carried it much farther and much higher than has been done by its brain-power, which alone has progressed. If there is no evolution for them here, do they develop elsewhere? What are those powers which exist outside and independent of the laws of this earth? Do they then belong to other worlds? But, if so, what are they doing in ours? One would sometimes think, at the sight of so much neglectfulness, uncertainty and inconsistency, that man's evolution had been intentionally retarded by a superior will, as though that will feared that he was going too fast, that he was anticipating some pre-

established order and moving prematurely
out of his appointed plane.

13

And the riddles accumulate which we
cannot hope to solve. It has been said that
these abnormal faculties are communications or infiltrations, themselves abnormal,
which have found their way through the
partitions that separate our consciousness
from our subconsciousness. This is very
likely, but it is only a minor side of the
question. It would be important before all
to know what that subconsciousness represents, whither it tends and with what it itself is communicating. Is the cerebral
form of knowledge a necessary or an acci-
dental stage? Is the impersonal form
which it takes in the subconsciousness the
only true one? Is there really, as everything seems to prove, a hopeless incompati-
bility between our intellectual faculties and

those faculties of uncertain origin, to such an extent that the latter are unable to manifest themselves except when the former are weakened or temporarily suspended? It has, at any rate, been observed that they are hardly ever exercised simultaneously. Are we to believe that, at a given moment, mankind or the genius that presides over its destinies had to make an exclusive and awful choice between cerebral energy and the mysterious forces of the subconsciousness and that we still find traces of its hesitations in our organism? What would have become of a race of men in which the subconsciousness had triumphed over the brain? Is not this the case with animals; and would not the race have remained purely animal? Or else would not this preponderance of a subconscious element more powerful than that of the animals and almost independent of our body have resulted in the disappearance of life as we know it; and should we not even now be leading the life which we shall probably lead when we are dead? Here are a number of questions to which there are no answers and which are nevertheless perhaps not so idle as one might at first believe.

14

Amidst this antagonism, whose triumph are we to hope for? Is any alliance between the two opposing forces for ever impossible so long as we are in the flesh? What are we to do meanwhile? If a choice be inevitable, which way will our choice incline; and which victim shall we sacrifice? Shall we listen to those who tell us that there is nothing more to be gained or learnt in those inhospitable regions where all our bewildering phenomena have been known since man first was man? Is it true that occultism—as it is very improperly called, for the knowledge which it

seeks is no more occult than any other—
is it true that occultism is marking time,
that it is becoming hopelessly entangled in
the same doubtful facts and that it has not
taken a single step forward since its rena-
scence more than fifty years ago? One must
be entirely ignorant of the wonderful efforts
of those fruitful years to venture upon
such an assertion. This is not the place to
discuss the question, which would require
full and careful treatment; but we may
safely say that until now there is no science
which in so short a time has brought order
out of such a chaos, ascertained, checked
and classified such a quantity of facts, or
more rapidly awakened, cultivated and
trained in man certain faculties which he
had never seriously been believed to possess; and furthermore none which has
caused to be recognized as incontestable
and thus introduced into the circle of the
realities whereon we base our lives a num-

ber of unlikely phenomena which had
hitherto been contemptuously passed over.
We are still, it is true, waiting for the do-
mestication of the new force, its practical
application to daily use. We are still waiting for the all-revealing, decisive manifestation which will remove our last doubts
and throw light upon the problem down to
its very source. But let us admit that we
are likewise waiting for this manifestation
in the great majority of sciences. In any
case, we are already in the presence of an
astonishing mass of well-weighed and verified materials which, until now, had been
taken for the refuse of dreams, fragments
of wild legends, meaningless and unimpor-
tant. For more than three centuries, the
science of electricity remained at very much
the same point at which our psychical
sciences stand to-day. Men were recording, accumulating, trying to interpret a host
of odd and futile phenomena, toying with

The Unknown Guest

Ramsden's machine, with Leyden jars, with Volta's rough battery. They thought that they had discovered an agreeable pastime, an ingenious plaything for the laboratory or study; and they had not the slightest suspicion that they were touching the sources of an universal, irresistible, inexhaustible power, invisibly present and active in all things, that would soon invade the surface of our globe. Nothing tells us that the psychic forces of which we are beginning to catch a glimpse have not similar surprises in store for us, with this difference, that we are here concerned with energies and mysteries which are loftier, grander and doubtless fraught with graver consequences, since they affect our eternal destinies, traverse alike our life and our death and extend beyond our planet.

15

It is not true therefore that the psychical

sciences have said their last word and that
we have nothing more to expect from them.
They have but just awakened or reawak-
ened; and, to postdate Guyau's prediction
by a hundred years, we might say, with
them in our minds, that the twentieth century "will end with discoveries as ill-formu-
lated but perhaps as important in the moral
world as those of Newton and Laplace in
the astronomical world." But, though we
have much to hope from them, that is no
reason why we should look to them for
everything and abandon in their favour
that which has brought us where we are.
The choice of which we spoke, between the
brain and the subconsciousness, has been
made long ago; and it is not our part to
make it over again. We are carried along
by a force acquired in the course of two or
three thousand years; and our methods, like
our intellectual habits, have of themselves
become transformed into a sort of minor

subconsciousness superposed upon the major subconsciousness and sometimes mingling with it. Henri Bergson, in his very fine presidential address to the Society for Psychical Research on the 28th of May, 1913, said that he had sometimes wondered what would have happened if modern science, instead of setting out from mathematics, instead of bringing all its forces to converge on the study of matter, had begun by the consideration of mind; if Kepler, Galileo and Newton, for instance, had been psychologists:

"We should certainly," said he, "have had a psychology of which to-day we can form no idea, any more than before Galileo we could have imagined what our physics would be; a psychology that probably would have been to our present psychology what our physics is to Aristotle's. Foreign to every mechanistic idea, not even conceiving the possibility of such an explanation, science would have enquired into, instead of dismissing *a priori,* facts such as those which you study; perhaps 'psychical research' would have stood out as its principal preoccupation. The most general laws of mental activity once discovered (as, in fact, the fundamental laws of mechanics were discovered), we should have passed from mind, properly so-called, to life; biology would have been constituted, but a vitalist biology, quite different from ours, which would have sought behind the sensible forms of living beings the inward, invisible force of which the sensible forms are the manifestations."

It would therefore in the very first days of its activity have encountered all these strange problems: telepathy, materializations, clairvoyance, miraculous cures, knowledge of the future, the possibility of survival, interplanetary intelligence and many others, which it has neglected hitherto and which, thanks to its neglect, are still in their infancy. But, as the human mind is not able to follow two diametrically opposite directions at the same time, it would necessarily have rejected the mathematical sciences. A steamship coming from another hemisphere, one in which men's minds had taken, unknown to ourselves, the road which our own has actually taken, would have seemed to us as wonderful, as incredible as the phenomena of our subconsciousness seem to us to-day. We should have gone very far in what at present we call the unknown or the occult; but we should have known hardly anything of physics, chemistry or mechanics, unless, which is very probable, we had come upon them by another road as we travelled round the occult. It is true that certain nations, the Hindus particularly, the Egyptians and perhaps the Incas, as well as others, in all probability, who have not left sufficient

traces, thus went to work the other way
and obtained nothing decisive. Is this
again a consequence of the hopeless incom-
patibility between the faculties of the brain
and those of the subconsciousness? Possibly; but we must not forget that we are
speaking of nations which never possessed
our intellectual habits, our passion for precision, for verification, for experimental
certainty; indeed, this passion has only
been fully developed in ourselves within
the last two or three centuries. It is
to be presumed therefore that the Euro-
pean would have gone much farther in the
other direction than the Oriental. Where
would he have arrived? Endowed with a
different brain, naturally clearer, more ex-
acting, more logical, less credulous, more
practical, closer to realities, more attentive
to details, but with the scientific side of his
intelligence uncultivated, would he have
gone astray or would he have met the truths

which we are still seeking and which may
well be more important than all our material conquests. Ill-prepared, ill-equipped,
ill-balanced, lacking the necessary ballast of
experiments and proofs, would he have
been exposed to the dangers familiar to all
the too-mystical nations? It is very difficult to imagine so. But the hour has now
perhaps come to try without risk what he
could not have done without grave peril.
While abandoning no whit of his understanding, which is small compared with the
boundless scope of the subconsciousness,
but which is sure, tried and docile, he can
now embark upon the great adventure and
try to do that which has not been done before. It is a matter of discovering the connecting link between the two forces. We
are still ignorant of the means of aiding,
encouraging, developing and taming the
greater of the two and of bringing it closer
to us; the quest will be the most difficult,

the most mysterious and, in certain respects, the most dangerous that mankind has ever undertaken. But we can say to ourselves, without fear of being very far wrong, that it is the best task at the moment. In any case, this is the first time since man has existed that he will be fronting the unknown with such good weapons, even as it is also the first time since its awakening that his intelligence, which has reached a summit from which it can understand almost everything, will at last receive help from outside and hear a voice that is something more than the echo of its own.

THE END